GOOD NEWS IN
LETTERS OF PAUL

Ephesians, Philippians, Colossians,
1 & 2 Thessalonians and *Philemon*
in Today's English Version

introduced by
DAVID H. C. READ

Collins
FONTANA BOOKS
in co-operation with The Bible Reading Fellowship

First published in Fontana Books 1975
© David H. C. Read 1975

Today's English Version of
Ephesians, Philippians, Colossians,
1 & 2 Thessalonians and *Philemon*
© American Bible Society, New York, 1966, 1971

Made and printed in Great Britain by
William Collins Sons & Co Ltd Glasgow

CONTENTS

PREFACE

Anyone who turns to the New Testament to discover what the Gospel – the Good News of Christ – really is will have to reckon with the letters of Paul. He takes up nearly as much space in the book as the combined works of the four evangelists and has left his imprint on the creeds, the prayers, and the hymns of the Church through the ages. There is clearly such a thing as 'The Good News according to Paul', and it is the purpose of this book to offer suggestions as to its main emphases and to stimulate further exploration.

Since Paul is venerated by many as the intrepid apostle to the Gentiles and the foremost exponent of the Gospel of grace, and detested by others as the perverter of the 'simple' message of Jesus, I would plead for a fresh and open-minded approach. My sympathies will be manifest: if I had not been captivated by the content of these letters and the personality who emerges from them, I should not have undertaken this little study. But I pray that those who find Paul unsympathetic, harsh, or obscure, will have another look at both the man and his writings.

The text used throughout (unless otherwise indicated) is that of Today's English Version. Those who are rooted in evangelical theology will miss old friends like 'justification' and 'sanctification' but will soon discover that the content of these words is not lost. In fact, it may be a stimulus to our fresh understanding to compare the new translation with familiar phrases from the King James Bible. Those to whom the whole field of Pauline thought is new, will, I trust, hear what he had to say as vividly as those who first read these letters in the language of their day.

This is not a book that requires a long list of acknowledgements of sources consulted. Since it is written from the heat of a busy parish life – they weren't, except for necessary checking on facts. But over the years I have been indebted to more scholars than could possibly be listed, and I have tried to keep in touch with recent literature in this field. There is, however, one book that has lived in my mind as a friend through the years and among the very few quotations in these pages are two from *A Man in Christ* by James S. Stewart.

The short introductions to the letters are intended to help the reader form an impression of when, where, and why each one was written. Since some matters of date, origin and authorship are still a subject of debate, I hope it will be understood that what I have chosen to print is by no means definitive.

Since Paul himself seems often to have used an amanuensis, it is fitting for me to express my indebtedness to my secretary, Carolyn Mathis, who so accurately interpreted my manuscript and, occasionally, my mind.

June 6, 1975   D.H.C.R.

1. THE MAN AND HIS AUDIENCE

It might be considered a concession to the modern mood to begin an enquiry into the letters of Paul with a look at the man himself. The thirst for biographical detail about a writer is a comparatively recent phenomenon. Even fifty years ago no one expected to find a book by Kipling or H. G. Wells with a photograph and potted biography on the dust-cover. Before that you didn't even expect a dust-cover, and any curiosity you might have about the life and habits of the author was strictly limited. What mattered then was the book and its contents, and no one worried about whether or not the author wore glasses and a beard, or speculated on the intimacies of his sex life. If you go back far enough I think you will discover that this lack of interest in the person of the writer meant that few were even worried about what we call 'authenticity' – the question of whether, for instance, William Shakespeare of Stratford-upon-Avon actually wrote the plays that bear his name. I remember my Greek teacher, when dealing with the authorship of the *Odyssey* and the *Iliad* quoting one of his professors to the effect that it didn't really matter very much whether they were written by Homer or by another gentleman of the same name.

'The play's the thing,' said Hamlet, and I would counter a lot of argument about the authorship of scriptural books by saying: 'The Bible's the thing.' If God speaks to me through something I find in what is called 'The Second Epistle of Peter' – a book which almost no one believes to have been written by the apostle, and about which even John Calvin had his doubts – I am not going to lose sleep over any feeling that I have been the victim of a literary trick. Every book of the Bible comes to us soaked in a long history of Church use and private piety, and while there is great gain for all of us in the labours of the scholars who have elucidated its composition, authorship, editing, and textual tradition, in the end it must make its own impression. So in offering some kind of running commentary on the letters of Paul I will not spend much time on the still-burning arguments as to which of the epistles that bear his name were actually written by him. For those interested let me just say that there is general agreement that the apostle actually wrote Romans, 1 and 2 Corinthians, Galatians, Philippians, Colossians, 1 and 2 Thessalonians, and Philemon. Some think Ephesians is by another hand and many that 1 and 2 Timothy and Titus come from some 'Paulinist' of a later time. Even computers are now brought into the debate on the questionable assumption that by establishing a programme of Paul's favourite words you can decide whether or not he wrote any particular letter. What seems to me evident is that the collection of letters that bears his name, whatever their difference in tone and detail, bear the stamp of his authority and reflect in their major emphases his interpretation of the Good News. The only point at which the question of authenticity could affect this study would be the evaluation of personal references. Since we are concentrating on Ephesians, Philippians, Colossians, Thessalonians, and Philemon (Romans and Corinthians are the subject of separate studies in this series) this question should not trouble us too much.

Why, then, should I preface this guide to these books by a look at the man and his audience? Would it not be better to concentrate on the contents of the letters, offering some clues to the understanding of words and ways of thought that raise difficulties for us today? The real reason for turning the spotlight on Paul himself before we work at a fresh understanding of his letters is not to pander to the modern taste for psychologizing and prying into the private lives of authors. It is simply that the letters themselves make it impossible to ignore the personality behind them. Few collections of literature anywhere bear such an impress of a dominant personality, and it is impossible to abstract them from the character and experiences of the man who wrote them. Students of Shakespeare know how precarious an undertaking it is to attempt to draw conclusions from the plays as to his attitude to life, or his political opinions, or religious convictions. So totally does he immerse himself in the characters of his creation that we are quite unable to find the real Shakespeare standing up. It is the opposite with Paul. Every line comes straight from his heart. 'I am certain . . .' (Romans 8:38) 'All I want is to know Christ . . .' (Philippians 3:10) 'I was made a servant of the Gospel by God's special gift' (Ephesians 3:7). 'For what is life? To me, it is Christ' (Philippians 1:21). 'With my own hand I write this: Greetings from Paul' (2 Thessalonians 3:17).

You cannot get away from the sound of this man's voice throbbing with his personal experience of the Good News. He writes with apostolic authority, sometimes using the 'royal we', but never approaches the cold objectivity of a modern ecclesiastical pronouncement. He even found it necessary on at least one occasion to insist that he was giving his own personal opinion. When speaking about Christians married to pagan wives he remarked: 'To the others I say (I, myself, not the Lord) . . . he must not divorce her' (1 Corinthians 7:12). Everywhere in these letters we hear the accents of a passionate Christian leader speaking from the heart and we cannot avoid being confronted by him, forming an impression of the man, and getting some idea of the kind of people to whom he was writing.

It is the neglect of this personal aspect of the letters that has led to many misunderstandings of their content, and made it hard for the ordinary reader to catch the echo of an enthusiastic witness for Christ telling how the Good News transforms the whole of life. Most of us have heard his writings in the form of brief extracts solemnly read as the 'Epistle' in the liturgy of the Church. As such they often appear to be somewhat laboured and complicated expositions of what is being said so much more clearly and simply in the Gospel readings. The worshipper tends to be left with the impression that, while Jesus comes through to us as a striking phrasemaker, and as the centre of a series of remarkable incidents, Paul is responsible for muddying the waters with philosophical abstractions and theological technicalities. 'I'll take Jesus, but you can keep Paul' is what many a layman wants to say to his pastor. When a real live letter is ripped into little sections and intoned in the cadences of sixteenth-century English something is apt to get lost – and something is a living, breathing, stimulating, warm-hearted, infectiously believing character called Paul of Tarsus.

In the same way the objectifying of Paul's letters – the habit of treating them as an anonymous, logically constructed, block of Christian doctrine – has had a dismal effect on the theology of the Church. I often think that there must be some corner of heaven where the apostle chuckles over the elaborate systems that have been erected on the basis of some remark that he threw out in the heat of the moment as he dictated a letter to his friends at Philippi or Rome. This game began not long after Paul's death. As with every great creator spirit along came a flock of disciples who tried to impose on the flaming insights of Christian genius their tepid systems and logical constructions. It happened to Luther. It happened to Calvin. It is, I believe, the reason that Karl Barth used to say: 'I am not a Barthian.' Some have even detected the beginnings of this process in the letters they consider to have been by a later hand, but it is certain that before many centuries had gone by the figure of the ardent ambassador of Christ had disappeared in a morass of scholasticism.

What Christians call the 'Word of God' comes to us through the intensely human words of very real human beings. Just as Jesus, whom the Church declares to be the living Word, God's ultimate disclosure of himself to mankind, was truly human and not some divine phantom visiting the earth, so the Bible writers through whom God speaks were truly human and not the automatic recorders of words dictated from the heavens. In no way are we detracting from the evident power of Paul's letters to convey the Word of God if we insist that they *are* real letters from a man whose portrait emerges, 'warts and all', from what he wrote, and that they were written to specific groups of people, or to individuals, who had their own peculiar needs and problems.

So the first clue to understanding these books is to discard any idea that they are a set of theological exercises, or sermons in cold storage, and approach them as letters written by a leader of the Christian Church in that exciting period between twenty and thirty years after the crucifixion. They are by far the earliest evidence we have about the Good News, since the Gospels came along about a generation later. We are, as it were, listening in to the conversations of the Church in its earliest years about the meaning of the news about Jesus that was transforming their lives and opening up new horizons of experience and thought. The conversations are, of course, dominated by the voice of Paul, but we learn, as we always do from letters that have been preserved, something about the people to whom they are addressed. We obviously do not have all the letters. (What we call 1 and 2 Corinthians are what remains of what was probably a very lengthy correspondence with a church that gave him more headaches than most.) If you object that few people today write letters that run to such length as some of Paul's, I would remind you, not only of your great-grandmothers, but of the fact that many of these were written from prison conditions which, as I can testify, leave plenty of time for the reflective scribbler. According to the custom of the day, these letters begin with the name of the writer, instead of our 'Dear So-and-so', and end with a salutation. What distinguishes Paul's letters from the pagan conventions is the Christianizing of the greetings and the salutations. 'From Paul,' he writes to the Corinthians, 'who by the will of God was called to be an apostle of Christ Jesus, and from our brother Sosthenes (nothing humanizes these letters so much as Paul's affectionate name-dropping in almost everything he wrote) – To the church of God which is in Corinth.' The Christianizing of a convention like this may have something to say to a generation that throws around words like 'dear', 'faithfully', and 'sincerely' indiscriminately, and for whom, in Britain, the tax-collector's threatening letter is signed 'your obedient servant'.

Letters are always prompted by some special occasion (even if it is only a desire to keep in contact or to thank for one's 'bread-and-butter') and Paul's were sped on their way nearly always by some emergency that had arisen. It helps a lot in our understanding if we can guess at what was particularly troubling him about the church or the person to whom he was writing. A simple example that can be studied in a moment is the letter to Philemon. Not much scholarship is needed to detect that this was a very intimate letter to a friend recommending, with a great deal of tact, that he receive back into his home a runaway slave who also happened to be a Christian.

There are indications all over the place that Paul often wrote, or dictated, at breathless speed. He interrupts himself, changes direction suddenly, breaks out with passionate asides, and is not above at times letting his mordant wit get the better of him. (In his furious argument against the party that wanted the Christians of Galatia to insist on circumcision as well as baptism the King James version tactfully obscures what he lets slip in what he has to say about the circumcisers: 'I wish that the people who are upsetting you would go all the way; let them go on and castrate themselves!' [Galatians 5:12].) The most touching moments in the letters are when his devotion to his loyal Christian friends comes through and when he breaks, as he often does, into sudden paeans of praise to the God and Father of Jesus Christ. Sometimes, when he gets into very deep waters as when in the letter to Rome he tries to fathom God's purpose for the Jewish people who have not accepted the Messiah, he throws up the theological sponge in an acknowledgement that the mystery is too much for him. 'My brothers, how I wish with all my heart that my own people might be saved!' is his cry, and then after pages of argument, he ends with a quote from the prophets: 'Who knows the mind of the Lord? Who is able to give him advice?' and then adds 'for all things were created by him, and all things exist through him and for him. To God be the glory for ever.' Then he picks up his pen to continue his exposition of the meaning of faith.

Real letters, then, from a very real person. And our next step should be to be ready to revise our views about this person. For most people approach the letters of Paul with some kind of prejudice, for or against the apostle. In my present church I know there are devoted admirers of Paul and that there are some who dislike him so much they would rather not hear so frequently about him from the lectern and the pulpit. There's nothing wrong in having preferences among the great figures of our Christian heritage. Talking about Paul and John, Archbishop Temple once noted that the great scholar Bishop Gore had said that he felt at home in the world of Paul, while paying occasional visits to the strange territory of John. Temple said that with him it was the other way around. If saints and scholars of the Church are allowed to have their prejudices, then no one should feel awkward about feeling less drawn to one Bible writer than another. What I would plead for, however, is an openness to the possibility that we may have been misinformed. Especially with this rugged apostle to the Gentiles there is a temptation to accept at second-hand certain popular prejudices.

For instance, it is often said that Paul was a cold-blooded intellectual who transformed the simple message of Jesus into an elaborate theology. Writer after writer in the secular world has transmitted this idea of an idyllic Jesus proclaiming an attractive Gospel of a loving God who asks us to love one another being seized upon by this Rabbinic scholar and made the object of fantastic theological speculation. For authors like Bernard Shaw, and his many successors, Paul is the great villain of the Christian religion, turning the simple faith *of* Jesus into a complicated faith *about* Jesus. Paul emerges from this treatment as a 'desiccated calculating machine', absorbed in his dogmatic constructions, and a total stranger to the love that Jesus taught and lived.

You don't need to read far in these letters to recognize the absurdity of this picture. Not only do they ring with the passion of a preacher whose theology is transmuted into life, but who has ever so magnificently caught the spirit of Jesus as the one who wrote the unsurpassed hymn to Christian love in the thirteenth chapter of the first letter to the Corinthians? Sure, there is theologizing in these letters, but not one of them closes without warm practical advice as to how to put the doctrine into practice through the Spirit of Christ. The man who could launch a diatribe against his opponents in Galatia with every intellectual device at his command wrote in that same letter that 'the Spirit produces love, joy, peace,

patience, kindness, goodness, faithfulness, humility, and
self-control.' The man who is supposed to be an arid
and dogmatic scholastic, absolutely sure that he had the
whole truth in his grasp, is the one who wrote: 'I do not
claim that I have . . . succeeded [in the Christ-like life]
or have already become perfect. I keep going on to try
to win the prize for which Christ Jesus has already
won me to himself. Of course, brothers, I really do not
think that I have already won it; the one thing I do,
however, is to forget what is behind me and do my best
to reach what is ahead.' Does that sound like a dogmatist
who has it all locked up?

Then there is an opposite prejudice about Paul which
takes another tack. This man, we are told, was an eastern
mystic, an *exalté*, who translated the moral teachings of
Jesus into a Christ-cult based on the ideas and practices
of the mystery religions that swarmed over that section
of the Roman Empire where he lived and operated. We
are thus invited to believe that he was not really an
intellectual, but the kind of person, with whom we are
so familiar today, who delights in mystic cults, in esoteric
religions, in abracadabra of all kinds, and is thrilled by
the feeling of being initiated into secret rites that the
ordinary world cannot penetrate or understand. We shall
discover that Paul was, of course, familiar with the
language and some of the customs associated with the
mysteries of Eleusis, Cybele, and Isis. Words like
'salvation' and 'resurrection' were used in these cults,
and ceremonies connected with the ideas of rebirth and
identification with a god or goddess. Some of these
were wild and corybantic, involving bloodshed and
delirium of various kinds. Others had been spiritualized
and initiated the worshipper into divine visions and
assurances of immortality. But it is one thing for a
Christian apostle to be aware of such mystery religions,
to share some of their vocabulary, to use their aspirations
as a point of contact for the proclamation of the Good
News. It is quite another for him to be engaged in
transforming the profoundly Jewish message of Jesus into
the kind of pagan religion that was anathema to all who
had been raised, as Paul and all the apostles were, in the
piety and ethical rigour of the Old Testament. Some of

the (to us) more obscure references in the letter to the
Colossians about 'special visions' and 'worship of angels'
(Colossians 2:18) probably had to do with his strenuous
attempt to keep ideas from these mystery religions from
infiltrating the Christian Church – and we would do well
to listen to his warnings today.

This is not to say that Paul was in no sense a mystic.
It is the thesis of this book that the central theme of the
Good News according to Paul is a union with Christ
that transforms all life, a union that cannot possibly be
expressed in purely rational terms. Paul even speaks of
rapturous mystical experience. 'I will now talk about
visions and revelations given me by the Lord. I know a
certain Christian man who fourteen years ago was
snatched up to the highest heaven (I do not know whether
this actually happened, or whether he had a vision – only
God knows). I repeat, I know that this man was snatched
to Paradise (again, I do not know whether this actually
happened, or whether it was a vision – only God knows),
and there he heard things which cannot be put into words,
things that human lips may not speak' (2 Corinthians
12:1-4). This fascinating passage (he may himself have
been the 'certain Christian man') speaks to me of a man
who recognizes the validity of mystical experience but
finds all he wants of it within the boundaries of his
Christian faith, and of a man who was unassuming and
hesitant in his judgement. In other words, he was neither
a flaming mystic, nor a dogmatic rationalist. The same
balance is to be observed in his treatment in the first
letter to Corinth of the phenomenon of glossolalia, or
'speaking with tongues'.

If we dismiss as caricature these contradictory portraits
of Paul as either a grimly intellectual systematizer, or
an ecstatic proponent of a new mystery religion, then we
are open to ask just who he was and how we can legiti-
mately form some impression of the man. The primary
source for what we can know about him remains these
letters. For I would emphasize again that they are the
earliest documents to be found in our New Testament
and bring us the first-hand testimony of a Christian
leader in the earliest days of the Church and a picture
of the kind of communities that had come into being as

a result of the preaching of the Good News. The fact
that Paul was writing in the middle of the first century
and was in contact not only with the churches he had
founded all over the Middle East but also with the
original church in Jerusalem makes it almost ludicrous
to suppose that he had totally defaced the message of
Jesus with no trace anywhere of any protest from Peter,
James, John, and the other disciples. The man who
emerges from these letters was clearly accepted by the
leaders of the Church as the bearer of the authentic
Good News, in spite of occasional clashes and differences
of opinion on detail.

There is, of course, another rich source for our understanding Paul. He is the dominant figure in the last
two-thirds of the book of the Acts of the Apostles. When
Luke decided to follow his account of Jesus with a sequel
on the story of the Church that bears his name there were
two main emphases in the narrative. The first was on the
actual launching of the Church as the new community
possessed by the Spirit of Christ and commissioned to
proclaim the Good News and continue his healing and
reconciling work. So we read about the strange happen-
ings at Pentecost and the subsequent adventures of the
new-born Church under the leadership of Peter. The
second emphasis (from chapter nine onwards) is on the
astonishing and unexpected spread of the Good News to
the Gentile world under the leadership of Paul. He comes
on the scene as a fanatical opponent of the followers of
Jesus who is literally bowled over by a vision of the risen
Christ and thereafter devotes himself to an astonishing
programme of Church expansion throughout the Roman
world. Since 'Acts' is one of the most readable and
enthralling books in the entire Bible many of us have
formed our portrait of Paul from its pages – Paul the
orator and debater, Paul the organizer, Paul the non-stop
missionary always on the move to claim new territory
for his Lord, Paul the diplomat, Paul the unyielding
prisoner, Paul the adventurer, Paul the undaunted in
face of enemies, brutalities, storms, and danger.

The book of the Acts fills in for us what lies behind
such an autobiographical aside as he gives us in a letter
to the Corinthians. In a rare moment of self-justification

he lashes out at his opponents who questioned his credentials as a Christian apostle: 'Are they Christ's servants? I sound like a madman – but I am a better servant than they are! I have worked much harder, I have been in prison more times, I have been whipped much more, and I have been near death more often. Five times I was given the thirty-nine lashes by the Jews; three times I was whipped by the Romans, and once I was stoned; I have been in three shipwrecks, and once spent twenty-four hours in the water. In my many travels I have been in danger from floods and from robbers, in danger from fellow Jews and from Gentiles; there have been dangers in the cities, dangers in the wilds, dangers on the high seas, and dangers from false friends. There has been work and toil; often I have gone without sleep; I have been hungry and thirsty; I have often been without enough food, shelter, or clothing. And, not to mention other things, every day I am under the pressure of my concern for all the churches.' You cannot go looking in the chapters of 'Acts' for exact confirmation of each of the adventures he mentions here but generally the picture coincides.

Since Luke was writing a generation after these letters of Paul were sent out we cannot expect to harmonize every detail of the story with every trait of character, but anyone setting out to read these epistles today should begin with a quick run through the narrative of 'Acts'. While some scholars are sceptical about some aspects of Luke's stories, suspecting him of tendentious writing to impress the Roman authorities, many believe he was working from extremely reliable sources and that in those passages where he uses the pronoun 'we' he was actually drawing upon a travel diary he kept as an actual companion of Paul on these journeys. It's a fascinating picture that opens up – the young Gentile doctor who finds himself caught up in the adventures of this Jewish preacher passionately devoted to another Jew he calls his Lord and Saviour.

When we put the pieces together what do we find as to the character of this extraordinary man who, more than others, is responsible for the fact that the Good News broke from the Palestinian swaddling-clothes to become by far the most widespread and influential religion the world has ever known? Like him, or detest him, no one can deny that it was his mental and spiritual courage in breaking with the confining ties that kept the nascent Gospel within the limits of Judaism, his moral and physical courage in braving powerful opponents on three sides – the Jewish hierarchy, the Roman establishment, the Greek culture – as well as constant sniping from within the churches that made possible the arrival of Christianity as a world-religion and its fantastic expansion throughout the world. What, we must wonder, could equip any human being for such an assignment? He himself would undoubtedly have answered by such a phrase as: 'I have the strength to face all conditions by the power that Christ gives me', but it is legitimate to look for those elements in his upbringing and training that were to be so mightily transformed by the Spirit of Christ.

He was born in Tarsus, a city of some importance as a cultural centre and focal point for traffic in that north-west corner of the Mediterranean where modern Turkey touches Syria. 'No mean city' – according to the familiar phrase from one of Paul's speeches in the book of the Acts. Paul was probably born about the same time as Jesus, although there is no evidence that the two ever met. We can guess that he was raised in comfortable circumstances since the family had the privilege of Roman citizenship and he himself had liberty to travel and study in other parts of the empire, but little is known about the precise circumstances of his upbringing.

What we do know, without a shadow of doubt, is that he was born and raised a Jew. He never ceased to rejoice and marvel in that fact and, even after his conversion to Christ, he constantly referred with pride and awe to his Jewish birth and training. Writing to the Philippians, and explaining why he had ceased to put his trust in external ceremonies such as circumcision for his salvation, he broke out passionately: 'If anyone thinks he can trust in external ceremonies, I have even more reason to feel that way. I was circumcised when I was a week old. I am an Israelite by birth, of the tribe of Benjamin, a pure-blooded Hebrew. So far as keeping the Jewish Law is concerned, I was a Pharisee . . .' (Philippians 3:4, 5) On another occasion he wrote: 'But if anyone dares to boast of something – I am talking like a fool – I will be just as daring. Are they Hebrews? So am I. Are they Israelites? So am I. Are they Abraham's descendants? So am I' (2 Corinthians 11:21, 22). It is perhaps something a Gentile can never fully understand but, whatever it is that makes a Jew proud to be a Jew, Paul had it.

What we have now to try to understand as we think of this world of Paul's activities and writings is that Jews were then neither confined for the most part to Palestine as they had been for centuries before nor were they living a kind of ghetto existence as they often had to do later in the Gentile world. For this period of history at least, Jews were not only scattered all over the civilized world but were almost universally respected, admired, and even envied. There was very little of the disease we have come to know as anti-Semitism in the Roman Empire at this time. The authorities were so impressed with the moral strength and character of this people that they made Judaism a *religio licita*, a permitted religion, and even exempted the Jews from such imperial ceremonies as would offend their religious laws. At a time of moral disintegration and widespread indulgence in every nameable and unnameable vice, the adherence of this people to such a code as the Ten Commandments gave them special status in the eyes of most decent people. And at a time when the ancient religions had lost their hold and most intelligent people were scornful of tales about the amorous activities of gods and goddesses there was something about this worship of the one, holy God that appealed enormously to great numbers of thoughtful Gentiles. Many of those attached themselves to synagogues without actually becoming Jews by faith and practice. They are the people referred to in the New Testament as 'God-fearers'. These were the people whom Paul found in many of the synagogues he visited and who were fertile ground for the Good News that he brought. Other Gentiles actually converted, were circumcised, often baptized, and became members of the Jewish community.

This Jewish community, however, was not entirely

homogeneous. The dispersion that had occurred naturally led to developments in thought and worship that were not acceptable to the Jews of Jerusalem and its immediate environment. Jews of the 'Diaspora', as it was called, naturally felt remote from the Temple and so a vigorous new kind of religious life centred on the synagogue. Then the pressure of Hellenism, the name given to the culture of Greek origin that dominated the empire at this time, was immense. As in our day, Jewish leaders were deeply concerned about the problem of assimilation and intermarriage. So, in a city like Tarsus (where the Jewish community was large – it was large in most of the great cities, with over a million in Alexandria alone) there would be those who made every effort to raise their children according to the traditions of their forefathers and even to send them, if possible, to Jerusalem to study at the feet of respected teachers of the law.

This happened to Paul. At some point, perhaps in his student years, he studied under the famous Gamaliel. According to the book of the Acts (22:2, 3) in a speech to the crowd on the steps of the Roman fortress in Jerusalem he began by saying: 'I am a Jew, born in Tarsus of Cilicia, but brought up here in Jerusalem as a student of Gamaliel. I received strict instruction in the Law of our ancestors . . .' Paul would remain a Jew of the Diaspora, never quite accepted by the strictly orthodox in Jerusalem, but he deliberately chose to soak himself in the strictest traditions of his faith and attach himself to the Pharisees who were the uncompromising Puritans of the Jewish tradition.

Paul was unquestionably a young man of deep religious conviction and firmly attached to the moral and ceremonial requirements of Judaism. This is worth remembering when we ponder the significance of the conversion on the Damascus road, which is recounted three times in 'Acts' and constantly obliquely referred to in the letters. It was most certainly not the kind of conversion that implies the turning of a liar, a drunkard, or a debauchee, into an upright and moral citizen. It was something else, and we shall have to consider that something else when we come to ask what Paul really meant by such terms as 'sin', 'grace', and the 'new life in Christ'.

But this picture of the deeply religious Paul must raise another question. How much would such a young man be influenced by the prevailing culture of Hellenism – its literature, its art, its habit of thought, and its manners? We cannot accept the caricature of an insufferable prig who despised the writings of a Plato, rejected the drama of a Sophocles and joined in none of the amusements and entertainments of his pagan companions. Apart from the fact that the book of the Acts shows him respecting local traditions, and addressing a sophisticated audience in Athens with all the elegance of a cultured Hellenist (even quoting from the Greek poets), the letters reveal a man who had some acquaintance with Stoic and Epicurean philosophy, wrote a vigorous and imaginative Greek, and was not above using similes and metaphors drawn not only from the military but from the games of the amphitheatre. His famous remark about becoming 'all things to all men' (1 Corinthians 9:22), and his word to the Romans that 'I have an obligation to all peoples, to the civilized and to the savage, to the educated and to the ignorant', reveal a man who was far from writing off the culture of the Hellenistic world as the lure of the devil.

The man who emerges from our perusal of his letters is thus a somewhat complicated character in whom many odd influences are at work, and it is not surprising that it is extremely difficult to assign him to any simple category of human being. He was an intellectual; yet communicated easily with all kinds of people, earned his living at times as a tent-maker (or leather-worker), was much more often on the open road than in the ivory tower, and in the crisis of a shipwreck showed more shrewdness and guts than any soldier or sailor on board. He was a brilliant and imaginative theologian; but often seemed much more concerned about the practical details of Christian ethics. He was extremely sensitive and emotional, easily stung by insult, quick to resent a betrayal or a sneak attack; but could be extraordinarily calm under pressure and ready to reach a compromise. This fiery spirit seemed to be strangely possessed by what he called 'God's peace, which is far beyond human understanding'. He could be both gentle and rough, poetic and argumentative, irritable and composed, tremendously exalted and deeply depressed. All this simply reveals that we are dealing with a real person and not some creation of a pious imagination such as he may appear at times in the stained glass of our churches. For which of us is not also a bundle of contradictions, and the strongest personalities are usually those we find most difficult to type-cast.

Can we come any closer? What about hints dropped here and there about his health, his looks, his prejudices? There is no portrait or written description to give us the features of the man. But he modestly suggests that he was not particularly attractive or impressive in his physical presence. He seems to have been sensitive to the charge made by some of his opponents in the Church that his correspondence was much more effective than his bodily presence. 'Someone will say,' he wrote to those irritating Corinthians, 'Paul's letters are severe and strong, but when he is with us in person he is weak, and his words are nothing!' He refutes the taunt but it obviously stung. On another occasion he reminds the Galatians of the first visit he made to them when he happened to be sick. 'But you did not despise or reject me, even though my physical condition was a great trial to you.' He went on: 'You would have taken out your own eyes, if you could, and given them to me.' This reference has been taken by some to indicate that he suffered from some form of eye disease that gave him a pathetic, or even ludicrous, appearance at times.

There is little doubt that he suffered from some physical affliction that was a great grief to him. Nowhere is he so frank about it as in the fascinating passage where he speaks about what the King James version calls his 'thorn in the flesh', which is a literal translation of the Greek. The translation we are using renders the passage like this: 'But to keep me from being puffed up with pride because of the wonderful things I saw, I was given a painful physical ailment, which acts as Satan's messenger to beat me and keep me from being proud. Three times I prayed to the Lord about this, and asked him to take it away. His answer was, "My grace is all you need; for my power is strongest when you are weak"' (2 Corinthians 12:7-9). This touching aside has perhaps brought more insight and strength to hard-pressed Christians than the most elaborate of his arguments. Was it ophthalmia? Or epilepsy, or malaria? We can't know but, whatever it was, it gave him not only physical pain but mental distress and embarrassment. How moving is his confession that his towering pride needed something to keep him humble!

Now we have to touch on the favourite topic of all who rummage into the private lives of authors. Was he married? What about his attitude to sex? How did he get along with women? Let me spare you any succulent speculations and simply say that he almost certainly was never married, had many female friends whom he highly respected as having 'worked hard with me to spread the gospel' (Philippians 4:3) like Priscilla who with Aquila her husband is called a 'fellow worker in the service of Christ Jesus' (Romans 16:3), and was limited in his advice on marriage by an expectation (at least in his earlier days) that the world was coming to an end in a very short time, and in his directions about woman's subordination in the home and in the Church by his strict training in the Judaism of his day.

It is comforting for those who are troubled by the apparent 'apostolic authority' given to Paul's statements about marriage that in one of his more unfortunate references (1 Corinthians 7) he says things like: 'I tell you this not as an order, but simply as a permission', 'I do not have a command from the Lord, but I give my opinion as one who by the Lord's mercy is worthy of trust', and he ends the whole passage by repeating: 'That is my opinion', adding rather weakly 'and I think that I too have God's Spirit.' It would seem that on this subject Paul is somewhat less than sure of himself. Perhaps this may have come from a realization of his lack of direct experience of the married state. 'Anyone who finds such difficulties in this question,' says Martin Dibelius in his book on Paul, 'has no first-hand experience of marriage. Paul was a bachelor not a widower.'

This is a brief glimpse of the Paul who has given us, quite unintentionally, these extraordinary letters that have found their way into our Bibles and nourished the

Christian faith of generation after generation. We should also keep in mind as we read that these were real people to whom he was writing, with specific questions, pressing fears and doubts, and a great desire to be strengthened in the faith. Their world was in some ways amazingly similar to ours today when so many familiar landmarks are disappearing, and when the Christian Church is threatened once more by the forces of paganism, secularism, superstition, and totalitarianism from without, and by all kinds of deviations and delusions from within. This is a time for the serious thinking and soaring faith, the sober stocktaking and joyful adventure, the sense of order and the sense of mystery, that are reflected in this practical mystic and warrior of Christ whom we call Paul of Tarsus.

2. HIS VISION OF CHRIST

If you can imagine yourself plunging into these letters of Paul for the first time without any kind of background in the Church or preconceptions about the man himself, what do you think would strike you most forcibly right away? My guess is that, before you had read more than a page or two, you would be saying to yourself: 'This man is totally obsessed by the person called Jesus Christ.' Within the Church this name is so continually sounded that its impact is dulled for us by repetition, and we can hear Paul's letters read without realizing how dominated he is by the figure of Jesus. Open the first letter to the Corinthians, and you will get some impression of how the recurrence of this name must strike anyone who is making his first acquaintance with the writings of Paul. In the first nine verses the name of Jesus Christ occurs ten times. Glance through the rest of this letter, and I doubt if you will find a single page where there is no reference to the one he calls his Lord.

'Jesus.' 'Jesus Christ.' 'Christ Jesus.' 'The Lord Jesus.' 'The Lord Jesus Christ.' He uses the names indiscriminately, and there is no need to try to find special significance in his choice at any one point in his writing. It seems to have been the practice of the early Church to speak of her Lord quite freely by using a number of names and titles. Later generations have developed all manner of quirks and customs about this. Some have found the plain word Jesus vaguely irreverent and insist on using some phrase like 'Our Blessed Lord'. 'Jesus' was, of course, the name given at his birth, and is simply the Greek version of the Hebrew name 'Joshua' which means 'Deliverer', and the apostles had no inhibitions about using it without decoration. 'Christ' is the Greek translation of 'Messiah' (or 'Anointed One') and, therefore, would not be used by his disciples until they had become convinced that Jesus, and no other, was the promised

Messiah. 'Jesus Christ' was thus a confession of faith.
At a decisive moment in the Gospels when Jesus asked
his disciples: 'Who do you say I am?' Peter answered:
'You are God's Messiah', and from that moment the
mark of a Christian was to confess that Jesus is the
Christ. 'Jesus Christ' is then more like a primitive creed
than a name and surname like 'John Smith'. It was only
about the time Paul's letters were written that the strict
meaning of 'the Christ' began to fade and Christians
used the names 'Jesus' and 'Christ' interchangeably. The
reason for this was that many of the Gentile Christians
were only vaguely aware of the original meaning of the
word. In modern times I have noticed that while preachers
refer often to 'Jesus' the average layman uses the name
'Christ'. (Recently, however, the name 'Jesus' has come
to the fore again as we read about 'Jesus people' and
the 'Jesus movement'.) For a while I tended in sermon
writing to use the word 'Jesus' when talking about the
historical character we read about in the Gospels and
'Christ' when I was referring to the risen and exalted
Lord who animates our Christian life today, but I have
given up this dubious distinction since it occurred to me
that I might be fostering the notion that 'Jesus' and
'Christ' are two very different beings – inducing, if I may
use the expression, a kind of Christological schizophrenia.

So let's forget the variations of name and title and
concentrate on what this fixation of Paul on the person
of Jesus really means. To get back into the picture we
have to remember that these letters are from one Christian
convert to other Christian converts within the new community that was being called the Church. The question
then is: What had happened to this devout Jew, raised
with Roman privileges, and influenced by Greek culture,
to make him centre his entire life around the person of a
young Palestinian who had been rejected by the religious
hierarchy and executed by the Romans as a potentially
dangerous agitator? That this was a drastic conversion
leading to a total reorientation of his whole life is evident
on every page of these letters. He uses the strongest
possible expressions to describe his utter devotion to
Jesus. 'For what is life?' he writes to the Philippians
(1:21). 'To me, it is Christ.' In the same letter he rejects

everything that he used to hold dear in his enthusiasm for his newly found Lord. 'I reckon everything as complete loss for the sake of what is so much more valuable, the knowledge of Christ Jesus my Lord. For his sake I have thrown everything away; I consider it all as mere garbage, so that I might gain Christ.' He could hardly put it more strongly than that, but there are passages in which he interprets this Christ-centredness almost in terms of his identity with his Lord. He told the Galatians (2:19-20), 'I have been put to death with Christ on his cross, so that it is no longer I who live, but it is Christ who lives in me. The life that I live now, I live by faith in the Son of God, who loved me and gave his life for me.' We shall have to return to this theme of mystical union with Christ at a later point. What matters now is the abundant evidence that for Paul Christianity was not a new set of doctrines to be added to his Judaism, or an attractive mystery religion that had weaned him away from the faith of his fathers. For him Christianity was Christ. It was devotion to him, new life in him, union with him. We are reading the living letters of what has been called a 'Christ-intoxicated man'.

Since nothing in his temperament or training and nothing in the subsequent impact of this man on the course of human history, gives us any excuse for writing him off as a religious fanatic, we have to listen to his testimony with the greatest respect. When I am asked why we should pay any more attention to Paul's claim to have found the secret and centre of human life than to any of the enthusiastic propagandists for cults and religions, new and old, my answer is that Paul's proclamation of the Good News of Christ Jesus must be recognized, whether you accept it or not, as having had an influence on our western world greater than any other after his Lord himself. His proclamation and interpretation of the Good News sent the name of Christ into our world as a revolutionary and life-changing force, and laid the foundation for a Christendom that survived the Roman Empire and for a constantly revitalized Church that has never ceased its expansion into all the world. In a quite extraordinary way this man's writings have sprung to life again with tremendous force at several points in the life of the Church. It was a verse from one of his letters that set Augustine on his way to become the dynamic intellectual and moral leader of the Church when the Roman Empire was crumbling, and with it a decadent Christianity. It was Paul's letters to the Romans and to the Galatians that opened the eyes of the monk Martin Luther to the real freedoms of the Gospel in another day of decadence and despair. It was a phrase from Paul that caused John Wesley's heart to be 'strangely warmed' and led to the evangelical tide that revived another lethargic Church. And it was in 1919, when the Churches were reeling from the effects of a devastating war and floundering in a sea of rationalism and relativism, that Karl Barth published his commentary on Paul's letter to the Romans and brought to the Churches the clarion call to hear again the Word of God – the Word he found in these letters of the apostle. I would want some such credentials as these from any apostle of a new Messiah or any evangelizing enthusiast of a new revelation. None of this is conclusive evidence that Paul has the truth, the whole truth, and nothing but the truth, but it is surely sufficient to win for him our respect and sympathetic hearing. This man who so influenced the minds and hearts of some of the greatest thinkers and leaders of our civilization is no fly-by-night fanatic whose Christ-obsession can be analysed by the psychologists of the abnormal.

The question then is: How did this sensitive, fiery, deeply religious Pharisee, this pillar of the local Roman establishment, this cultured product of a Hellenist civilization, arrive at a faith whose burning centre was the person of Jesus of Nazareth, a relatively obscure contemporary who had been crucified? The answer is given by Luke in the story of a vision of the living Christ, a revelation of such intensity that Paul was stunned, blinded, and out of action for three days after which he was restored to sight by a Christian in Damascus, and baptized into the Church.

In the meantime Saul kept up his violent threats of murder against the disciples of the Lord. He went to the High Priest and asked for letters of introduction to the Jewish synagogues in Damascus, so that if he should find any followers of the Way of the Lord there, he would be able to arrest them, both men and women, and take them back to Jerusalem.

On his way to Damascus, as he came near the city, a light from the sky suddenly flashed all around him. He fell to the ground and heard a voice saying to him, 'Saul, Saul! Why do you persecute me?' 'Who are you, Lord?' he asked. 'I am Jesus, whom you persecute,' the voice said. 'But get up and go into the city, where you will be told what you must do.' Now the men who were travelling with Saul had stopped, not saying a word; they heard the voice but could not see anyone. Saul got up from the ground and opened his eyes, but could not see a thing. So they took him by the hand and led him into Damascus. For three days he was not able to see, and during that time he did not eat or drink anything.

There was a disciple in Damascus named Ananias. He had a vision, in which the Lord said to him, 'Ananias!' 'Here I am, Lord,' he answered. The Lord said to him: 'Get ready and go to Straight Street, and in the house of Judas ask for a man from Tarsus named Saul. He is praying, and in a vision he saw a man named Ananias come in and place his hands on him so that he might see again.' Ananias answered: 'Lord, many people have told me about this man, about all the terrible things he has done to your people in Jerusalem. And he has come to Damascus with authority from the chief priests to arrest all who call on your name.' The Lord said to him: 'Go, for I have chosen him to serve me, to make my name known to Gentiles and kings, and to the people of Israel. And I myself will show him all that he must suffer for my sake.'

So Ananias went, entered the house and placed his hands on Saul. 'Brother Saul,' he said, 'the Lord has sent me – Jesus himself, whom you saw on the road as you were coming here. He sent me so that you might see again and be filled with the Holy Spirit.' At once something like fish scales fell from Saul's eyes and he was able to see again. He stood up and was baptized; and after he had eaten, his strength came back.

Acts:9:1-19

This story of dramatic conversion on the Damascus road is recounted on two other occasions in Acts, each time in the first person by Paul himself. In none of the letters does he specifically mention the time and place of this vision of Christ, although he makes it clear that both his Christian experience and his apostolic call were determined by an overwhelming personal encounter with the risen Christ.

For the understanding of these letters we have to keep in mind that Paul was always writing from the standpoint of one for whom Christianity was, in the first place, neither a new set of beliefs to be added to the traditions of Judaism nor a kind of religious club that kept alive the memory of Jesus, but a new life engendered by an encounter with the Son of God and sustained by the communion of those who shared this experience, a community so intimately related to the living Lord that he could call it the 'Body of Christ'. 'When anyone is joined in Christ,' he wrote (2 Corinthians 5:17), 'he is a new being; the old is gone, the new has come.' To the Colossians he wrote: 'He is the head of his body, the church; he is the source of the body's life.' Everything, then, centred on the reality of Christ who revealed himself as the Son of God, the Deliverer from sin and death, one who could be known both individually and in the communion of his Church. Being 'in Christ', 'joined to Christ', is for him the supreme kind of knowing that lights up the whole of life. It is not knowing *about* Christ – knowledge by information or reputation, but knowing *him* – knowledge by acquaintance. Thus he can say: 'All I want is to know Christ and to experience the power of his resurrection; to share in his sufferings and become like him in his death.' (Philippians 3:10)

We have then to ask: How is this Christ of Paul's vision related to the Jesus we read about in the Gospels? Are we hearing from a mystic who lives by a vision of the divine Saviour who may not really be identical with the young teacher who gave us the parables and the Sermon on the Mount, and was disposed of by the civil and religious establishment? Such questions may not be asked by those who have been raised in an evangelical tradition that assumed an identity between the Jesus of the Gospels and the Christ of Paul's vision. But anyone coming to the New Testament for the first time is bound to feel some tension between their picture of Jesus derived from the Gospels (at least the first three) and the Christ who is for Paul an inward spiritual force ('how very great is his power at work in us who believe', Ephesians 1:19) and the ultimate head of the universe ('God created the whole universe through him and for him', Colossians 1:16). It is not at first sight surprising that theories have been spun in almost every generation about a 'Paulinism' that is quite a different religion from the teachings of Jesus.

First we have to deal with the validity of mystical experience in the framework of religion. It is much easier now for the average reader to accept, if not to understand, the kind of vision that came to Paul on the Damascus road. A recent survey startled the pragmatic secularism of modern sociology, psychology, and some schools of theology by revealing that over half of the adults in the USA today would claim to have had some genuine mystical experience. Apparently in our so-called scientific age most people still believe that some kind of vision or illumination may come in which meaning, purpose, and a sense of peace and joy take possession of the soul. Whatever conclusions may be reached by a study of this phenomenon we are certainly living in times when the realm of the spirit is increasingly recognized as all-important, and 'supernatural' is ceasing to be a dirty word.

Paul, then, had a vision. Was it something that came, as it were, 'out of the blue' – the kind of thing that I read about nearly every week in the letters I receive from people who are convinced that to them has been revealed some ultimate truth never before made known to man? The story in 'Acts' contradicts any notion that Paul had been grasped by such a totally new and unrelated private revelation. Luke tells us that he heard a voice saying: 'Saul, Saul, why do you persecute me?' and that when he asked: 'Who are you, Lord?' the reply came: 'I am Jesus, whom you persecute.' It is impossible to demand that an account of a mystical experience like this should be written in the plain prose of a newspaper report any more than we should expect the light that flashed from the sky to be analysable by a light-meter. Exactly what happened on that road can no more be determined than what happened on the mountain of Jesus' transfiguration. But the story leaves no doubt whatever that it was Jesus who was the centre of this vision – and Paul knew very well who this Jesus was since he was engaged at that very moment in the persecution of his followers. It's absurd to ask, as some have done, how Paul could have recognized a person he had never seen. It was the instinctive recognition in his mind and conscience of one about whom he must have been constantly thinking during those past months. The form of the question also gives us another link with the real world around him. For he apparently realized that he had indeed been persecuting this Jesus he had never met by his persecution of his Church. This was no detached and private vision granted to a man about to found a new religion. It is Jesus whom we hear about, and Jesus was then the name of one who had very recently been alive and active in the Jerusalem Paul knew so well.

Another distinctive note of the story of Paul's vision is this dialogue that Luke reports. It is typical of the few visions reported in the Bible that they contain words, and not just pictures and symbols. The vision of the young Isaiah in the Temple (Isaiah 6) with its rich imagery of smoke and fire and winged creatures culminates in the dialogue: 'Whom shall I send . . . Lord, here am I; send me.' So here the imagery of the flashing light is merely incidental to the decisive word: 'Get up and go into the city, where you will be told what you must do.' Biblical visions are not for private enjoyment: they are always a summons to respond to the Word of God. So we are on safer ground in relating this vision of Paul's to the prophetic experience in the Old Testament than to any mystical illumination of a mystery cult.

But we must return to the letters where there is no specific reference to the Damascus road. In what way do we find Paul speaking of this decisive encounter, and what evidence is there that the Christ of whom he speaks so constantly and fervently was indeed the Jesus whose Church he has been persecuting?

One of the most important and illuminating passages that speak of Paul's decisive experience is to be found near the beginning of his letter to the Galatians. In that letter, as we shall see later, he had to defend his apostolic authority against those who considered him an upstart who was wrecking the good work of the Lord's original disciples by his ultra-liberal views concerning the reception of Gentiles into the Church. So he bluntly declares that there was nothing second-hand about his call to be an apostle of Jesus Christ and a herald of the Good News. 'Let me tell you, my brothers, that the gospel I preach was not made by man. I did not receive it from any man, nor did anyone teach it to me. Instead, it was Jesus Christ himself who revealed it to me.' At first sight this might be taken as a confession that his Gospel was indeed different from that preached by the disciples, and a rather presumptuous claim to have had a private revelation. That this would be a misunderstanding is clearly indicated by the decisive words to the Corinthians (1 Corinthians 15:3-8): 'I passed on to you what I received, which is of the greatest importance: that Christ died for our sins, as written in the Scriptures; that he was buried, and raised to life on the third day, as written in the Scriptures; that he appeared to Peter, and then to all twelve apostles. Then he appeared to more than five hundred of his followers at once, most of whom are still alive, although some have died. Then he appeared to James, and then to all the apostles. Last of all he appeared also to me – even though I am like one who was born in a most unusual way.'

That is a key passage to have in mind when reading claims to independence such as this one in the Galatian letter. What he is saying to the Galatians is not that he, as it were, invented the Gospel through a private revelation, but that his vision of Christ was at first hand, and his commission to declare the Good News a direct command of the Lord. Nothing in the letters gives room for supposing that Paul did not share the central themes of the Gospel with the leaders of the early Church. He was no schismatic, arrogantly disclaiming the authority of the accepted message of the Church. This alone makes it impossible to conclude that Paul's vision of Christ had little or nothing to do with the story of Jesus as recounted by the evangelists.

His description to the Galatians (1:15 ff.) of what happened to him at his conversion and during the years immediately following helps us to locate his vision of Christ firmly in the context of the Biblical tradition and the new community of Christians. After speaking again about his total dedication to the Jewish tradition ('I was ahead of most fellow Jews of my age in the practice of the Jewish religion. I was much more devoted to the traditions of our ancestors') he goes on: 'But God, in his grace, chose me even before I was born, and called me to serve him.' He is thus linking his encounter with the living Christ to the God he had worshipped from childhood. This disposes of any notion that Paul had discovered a new God called 'Christ', a mystical figure whom he now proclaimed to be the real Lord in the manner of the proponents of the new mystery religions. The Christ he had met on the Damascus road was revealed to him, he says, by the grace of the God of his fathers, and he even declares that this had been the purpose of the Eternal before he had ever been born. In this majestic way he refutes any suspicion that he has broken with the God revealed in the Old Testament Scriptures, or that his Christ is a new and rival deity. The next phrase is enormously important for understanding Paul's vision of Christ – 'when he decided to reveal his Son to me'. That, in his own words, is what happened on the Damascus road. It was not an intoxicating new discovery that he had made by virtue of his own mystical genius. It was not a sudden conversion to a new god and a repudiation of all the story of Israel. It was not the private appearance of Christ who was only vaguely related to the Jesus of the early Church. God, the eternal God of his fathers, the creator of heaven and earth, was the one who 'decided to reveal his Son to me'. And why? 'so that I might preach the Good News about him to the Gentiles'.

He goes on to speak about his relative isolation for some years, stressing the fact that he didn't ask to have his apostolate confirmed by the others. But he does admit that he had contact with those who were already pro-

claiming the Good News. 'It was three years later that
I went to Jerusalem to get information from Peter, and
I stayed with him for two weeks.' Can you imagine Peter
tolerating for two weeks the conversation of some fanatic
babbling about a Christ that Peter could not recognize?
'I did not see any other apostle except James, the Lord's
brother.' It is surely too much to be asked to believe
that a man who had talked with the brother of Jesus
himself was busy proclaiming some mythical Christ with
no resemblance to the figure in the Gospels.

A reader of the letters may indeed be puzzled by what
seems a scarcity of reference to events in the life of Jesus
and quotations from his teachings. It is this that has
led to the hasty conclusion that Paul's Christ was only
vaguely related to the Jesus of the Gospels. What we
have to remember is that these letters were going to
churches where almost certainly stories about Jesus and
extracts from his teaching were regularly read at services
of worship. Although the Gospels were still a long way
from assuming their final written form the Christian
communities were nourished by the material they contain. The habit that has become traditional in churches
that take their liturgy seriously of reading from the Old
Testament, the Epistles, and then the Gospels was
probably already taking root. Therefore not only did
the early Christians retain their strong roots in the Book
of the Law and the Prophets, but would listen to apostolic
letters like Paul's in the context of vivid reminders of the
events and sayings that are now recorded in the Gospels.
A perceptive reader will also catch constant echoes in
Paul's writings of the life and teachings of Jesus. It is
interesting that in the Book of Acts Paul is reported as
citing a saying of Jesus that is not included in any of our
Gospels: 'There is more happiness in giving than in
receiving.' Whenever Paul spells out the kind of life that
results from being 'in Christ', or filled with his Spirit,
we know at once that he is speaking of the impression
made by the historical character of Jesus depicted in the
Gospels. And, as has often been noted, his hymn to love
in the first letter to the Corinthians is nothing less than
a portrait of him.

In a somewhat puzzling passage (2 Corinthians 5:16)

Paul indicates perhaps why he does not concentrate on
the records of the human life of Jesus. He has been
speaking of how Christ 'died for all men so that those
who live should no longer live for themselves, but only
for him who died and was raised to life for their sake',
and he is going on to celebrate the 'new being' that is
ours in Christ (2 Corinthians 5:15-17). He interposes
the remark that 'no longer, then, do we judge anyone
by human standards. Even if at one time we judged
Christ according to human standards, we no longer do
so.' For 'according to human standards' the King James
Bible gives us the literal translation 'after the flesh'. (This
word 'flesh' is one of the key words we shall have to
examine later. Meantime 'according to human standards'
serves to illuminate this passage.) It seems to me that he
is reminding us that the Christian approaches the question
of the personality of Jesus with different standards from
those of the world outside, and is warning us against an
attempt to focus on the human personality of Jesus in
such a way as to construct some kind of hero-figure who
can be placed alongside others in the human story. He
is not brushing aside the contents of the Gospels as of
little importance compared with the exalted Christ in
whom he now believes, but confessing that before his
encounter on the Damascus road he had a totally
'human' view of Christ that led him astray. It could be
that he is warning us against the attempt to supplement
the Gospels with some biography of Jesus constructed
like any other 'Life' of a great man. There have been
innumerable such 'Lives' of Jesus in the last hundred
years. Some are useful and faithful to the Gospel material;
others are more imaginative, for good or ill, but it is
notorious that none have been successful. They nearly
always tell us more about the beliefs and prejudices of
the author than they do about Jesus. May it not be that
there is great wisdom in the liturgical practice of the
Church whereby the reading of the Epistle comes before
the reading of the Gospel? For this means that it is when
we have been reminded of the actual presence of the
living Christ in our hearts and in his Church that we are
enabled really to hear the Jesus of the Gospels and see
what was really happening. The Fourth Gospel, which is

a kind of link between the Synoptics and the Epistles, gives us a clue to this process when it constantly speaks of 'seeing his glory' while describing the most down-to-earth details of the events of Jesus' life.

The more closely we look at the references in these letters to the Christ who possessed him the more we feel the need for some alternative to the word 'vision'. I am using it because it expresses the dynamic inwardness of Paul's relationship with Jesus, but he himself uses the word only once, and then to express what he obviously regarded as a possible by-product of Christian faith. Before he speaks of the mysterious 'certain Christian' (who was probably himself) being 'snatched up to the highest heaven' and hearing 'things which cannot be put into words' (2 Corinthians 12:1-6) he makes the curious remark, 'I have to boast, even though it doesn't do any good. But I will now talk about visions and revelations given me by the Lord.' We learn a good deal about his private opinions and experience whenever he starts out with this 'I don't want to boast but . . .' formula. And here he seems to think of visions as occasional gifts received by a few Christians, rather in the same way as 'speaking with tongues'. He probably would not have described his experience on the Damascus road as a vision. The Gospels do not refer to the appearances of the risen Christ to his disciples as visions and he makes it plain that he considers his encounter to be the same as theirs. We cannot properly understand his writings unless we accept the fact that Paul was utterly convinced that Jesus was really alive, the same Jesus whose followers he had persecuted. The Resurrection as a fact of history as well as a spiritual triumph dominates everything he has to say about the Christian faith.

If we continue to use the word 'vision' it must only be as a convenient word to indicate that for Paul, and all who have heard the Good News through him, contact with Jesus is infinitely more than the remembrance of a holy life. It means a present life-changing power – what he calls 'God's power to save all who believe' (Romans 1:16) and 'the power working in us' (Ephesians 3:20). Vision thus refers to the inward eye that enables us to perceive who Jesus really is, and Paul prefers to use the great Christian words 'faith', 'hope' and 'love'. It will help us to understand the constant references in these letters to this dynamic presence of Christ if we note some emphases that clearly indicate that he is not talking about something recondite and mystical that is granted only to a few choice spirits.

(1) He never suggests, even in passing, that he has attained his vision of Christ by virtue of his exceptional talent or insight, or that he is interested in establishing a new Pauline cult. In this he differs from visionaries and founders of new religions both in his day and ours. Every time he writes about his own, or others', experience of the risen Christ, he talks almost exclusively about the grace of God. It is by God's grace and not his mystical skills or special piety that the vision comes. The most powerful statement of this truth is in his tremendous statement to the Corinthians when after declaring that 'It is not ourselves we preach; we preach Jesus Christ as Lord, and ourselves as your servants for Jesus' sake', he goes on: 'The God who said, "Out of darkness the light shall shine!" is the same God who made his light shine in our hearts, to bring us the light of God's glory, shining in the face of Christ.' (2 Corinthians 4:6)

Dr J. S. Stewart, commenting on this passage as a reflection on what happened to Paul himself on the Damascus road, has this to say: 'Something had happened comparable only to the great *Fiat Lux* of creation's dawn . . . To me, says Paul in effect, it was just like that – sheer miracle, a word proceeding out of the mouth of God, a creative act of omnipotence. To me, it was the birth of light and order and purpose and beauty, the ending of chaos and ancient night. And to me, as at that first creation, the morning stars sang together, and all the sons of God shouted for joy. God who said, "Let there be light," has shone within my heart; he has scorched me with his splendour, and remade me by his strength; and I now walk for ever in a marvellous light – the light of the knowledge of the glory of God in the face of Jesus Christ' (*A Man in Christ*, p. 82).

For Paul, not only his conversion but every step in his Christian life is dependent on this overwhelming grace of God, and in no way on his success as a mystic or a saint. For him it is always God first, Christ first, the Spirit first – and all else revolves around this trinitarian revelation of the love of God. Even when he tells the Philippians (2:12) to 'keep on working, with fear and trembling, to complete your salvation' he adds at once 'because God is always at work in you to make you willing and able to obey his own purpose.' The emphasis is never on Paul's, or our, capacity for 'seeing the invisible' but always on the Christ who is disclosed to us by the eternal God.

(2) Another distinctive feature of the kind of vision Paul is talking about in his letters is that it has the strongest moral implications. Mystical experiences such as we hear of today often seem to have little to do with ethics. The vision is enjoyed for its own sake, and for the sense of peace and well-being that it induces. Some of the more popular types of mysticism, including the instant mysticism of the drug, seem to be offered today rather as an escape from our responsibilities than as a moral stimulant. Paul's vision of Christ came in the first place, as we have seen, with a word of command that sent him out in a totally new direction. His continuing vision, which he describes by the haunting phrase 'in Christ', meant nothing less than a growing conformity to the mind, will, and character of his Lord. 'For we are ruled by Christ's love for us,' he writes (2 Corinthians 5:14). This is what he continually tells his Christian friends. 'The attitude you should have is the one that Christ Jesus had,' he wrote and then proceeds to a great hymn celebrating the humility and obedience of Jesus (Philippians 2:5 ff.).

In every letter to the churches his explication of the meaning of the Christian vision, of the union with Christ in his death and resurrection, of the inner working of the Spirit, is followed by a series of sharp and explicit admonitions about Christian behaviour in all kinds of circumstances. The indicatives of his exposition of the Good News, such as 'God, who through Christ changed us from enemies into his friends', pass almost at once into the imperatives of the new life – this God 'gave us the task of making others his friends also'. His is always the vision of the Christ who says: 'I love you just as the

Father loves me; *remain* in my love', and commands us to love one another. To be 'in Christ' is for Paul not so much a matter of enjoying an experience of glowing contact with the divine, and of 'joy and peace in believing', though it certainly was that, as of being energized from within to live and act as a true disciple.

(3) We cannot study these letters without being aware of another aspect of his vision that makes it very different from the typical mystical experience. There is something profoundly personal and private about the visions that have been reported right down to the present day. They are experienced by one solitary man or woman as a very intimate revelation from the divine dimension. And sometimes they are reported in such a way as to imply: 'I can't expect *you*, or anyone else, to understand.' The remarkable thing about Paul's vision of Christ is that, while it *was* intensely personal, and there is no doubt whatever about the blazing originality, even eccentricity, of this man, he never once speaks as though his experience of being 'in Christ' was an exclusive revelation beyond the reach of others. In fact, the commanding vision of the Damascus road drove him right out to share the Good News and offer to every man and woman the invitation to be 'in Christ'.

A glance at the salutations in the opening verses of his letters will reveal how profoundly he shared this sense of being 'in Christ' with those to whom he wrote. 'To the church of God which is in Corinth, to all who are called to be God's holy people, who belong to him in union with Christ Jesus . . .' (1 Corinthians 1:2) 'To God's people who live in Ephesus, those who are faithful in their life in Jesus Christ . . .' (Ephesians 1:1) 'To God's people in Colossae, those who are our faithful brothers in Christ . . .' (Colossians 1:2) 'To the people of the church in Thessalonica, who belong to God the Father and the Lord Jesus Christ . . .' (1 Thessalonians 1:1) We cannot suppose that all these people, who were drawn from every section of society, were what we would call natural mystics. As in any church today there would be a mixture of the visionary and the practical, the intellectual and the simple, the enthusiastic and the cautious. His vision of the Saviour and his Church embraced them all. One of the paradoxes that sparkles in these letters is the insistence of this man, whose personality was towering and whose individuality is stamped on every page, that 'we are all members together in the body of Christ' (Ephesians 4:25). 'There is no difference,' he wrote to the Galatians, 'between Jews and Gentiles, between slaves and free men, between men and women; you are all one in union with Christ Jesus.' These liberating words reveal how far he was from any private, esoteric, mystical vision of Christ.

'In Christ'. These little words contain the essence of the Good News for Paul, for himself and for all. No one can finish a reading of his letters without pondering what they can mean. They are unique in the history of religion, and even without parallel elsewhere in the New Testament. No one has ever spoken of being 'in Moses', or 'in Mohammed', or 'in the Buddha'. The nearest parallel in the New Testament is in the writings of 'John', especially the image of the vine and the branches (John 15:1 ff.). Thus it cannot be said that Paul was fostering a new kind of Christ-cult. He simply chose this way of expressing what has always been at the heart of the Good News – that a man or woman, of any race, religion, temperament, colour, or upbringing, can be laid hold of by God in such a way that they are drawn into an intimate, personal, and yet profoundly shared, communion with his Son, the crucified and living Christ, and experience the moral and spiritual dynamic of his Spirit. Thus for Paul the Good News must be interpreted not as primarily a message to be received by the mind but as a transforming friendship to which the nearest parallel is the intimate union of two human beings in love.

3. THE KEY WORDS OF HIS GOSPEL

The expression 'key words' is used with some hesitation in this chapter. It is not meant to suggest that there is a set of simple concepts which will immediately open up for you all the mysteries that lie hidden in these letters. From our glance at the nature of Paul's correspondence and the kind of man he was, it will be apparent that we are not dealing with esoteric and arcane teachings whose meaning has to be unlocked. Beware of the book that ignores the labours of two thousand years of scholarship and devotion and offers you some new key that will finally explain the Scriptures. Anyone can read Paul's letters in a good modern translation like Today's English Version and be drawn into an understanding and acceptance of the Christian Gospel without the intrusion of anyone jingling a set of theological keys. After all, Paul is talking about God, about Jesus Christ, and to people like you and me.

What may be helpful, however, is to have a look at one or two words that keep recurring in these letters since they provide powerful clues to his understanding of the Good News. Since Paul was not writing in either Elizabethan or modern English, and since all words and expressions have a way of changing meaning or collecting new associations over the years, it could be both useful and fascinating to try to discover what he really had in mind when he set down words like 'faith', 'grace', or 'love' – let alone the resounding polysyllables that have haunted books on Pauline theology for centuries, 'righteousness', 'justification', 'sanctification'. (Even where these big words have disappeared in a modern translation we have to ask if what has replaced them is really saying the same thing.)

It is commonplace that a word may change meaning completely over the years. When the King James Bible translated a phrase of the apostle James with 'superfluity of naughtiness', we might form a mental image of a turbulent kindergarten. What James was saying comes out in Today's English Version as 'wicked conduct'. The Greek is an ugly little word that is as vicious as it sounds. 'Naughty' formerly had that meaning. We may think we are hearing the right word when in the King James text we hear Paul warning Timothy (2 Timothy 3:6) about evil men who 'lead captive silly women laden with sins', but the word 'silly' then meant 'weak' or 'humble' – as when the above-mentioned King James VI once described himself as 'God's silly vassal'. We hardly need to be reminded that the collect which opens 'Prevent us, O Lord' is asking God to go before us and not to stop us, and that the word 'charity' has acquired meanings unknown to those who used it in Paul's celebration of *agape* in his letter to the Corinthians.

It might seem that this change of language has been taken care of by these new translations that are now circulating so widely. But this is a task that never ends. (It occurred to me when I quoted Paul's autobiographical passage including the words 'once I was stoned' that a new translator might have to find yet another word!) What matters more for our purpose is the associations, or colouring, that words acquire in varied times and circumstances. Especially in Church circles, certain words and phrases set off a chain reaction of thoughts and emotions prompted by experiences over the years. For instance the verse of Cowper's hymn that reads:

There is a fountain filled with blood,
Drawn from Emmanuel's veins;
And sinners plunged beneath that flood,
Lose all their guilty stains

could be sung with passionate fervour and conviction by one deeply rooted in an evangelical theology, while to the average member of our secular culture today it would sound not only incomprehensible but revolting.

Since Paul undoubtedly used words that were for him soaked in associations from his Jewish background, and others that had overtones from Greek culture and philosophy, we may have to dig below the surface to come close to what he is really saying. We may even have to rid ourselves of assumptions we have acquired from our own religious training if we had any. It is possible that one who comes fresh to these letters from a totally non-church background may hear better at times what the apostle is saying than those of us who have had certain interpretations dinned into our ears from childhood. In any case it is good to rummage around a bit to get hold of the sense in which Paul is using some quite familiar words.

We have already done this to some extent in pondering the meaning for him of the central point in his theology – Jesus Christ, and the expression that summarizes his Good News: 'in Christ.' We have seen that even those familiar words are soaked in an unfathomable sea of meaning deriving from the overwhelming impact of his vision of Jesus.

Whatever Paul is writing about in these letters there is one theme that is never very far away. It has to do with what the modern evangelist calls 'getting right with God'. So we might begin with a look at the expressions he uses when talking about the nature and demands of God and how human beings are related to him. It will be obvious even to the most casual reader that, although there is a mystical strain in Paul's religion, he is totally out of tune with the kind of mysticism that merges the human and the divine, and speaks of the basic unity of God and man. With his strong Old Testament background for him God remains God – the holy, the transcendent, the righteous, the Lord Almighty, the Creator – and man remains man – the created, the fragile, the dependent and (worse) the unrighteous, the sinner. (That's a word we shall have to return to.) He assumes such a chasm between man and God that he can say to Christian converts about their former life: 'In the past you were spiritually dead because of your disobedience and sins.' (Ephesians 2:1) He tells others (Colossians 1:21) 'At one time you were far away from God and were his enemies because of evil things you did and thought.' We cannot understand the passion with which he proclaims the Good News of reconciliation, of 'peace with God' unless we realize how profoundly he felt this alienation of man from the holy God. This may be one of the most serious difficulties for the modern reader, since much popular religion today is built on the virtual identification of God and man, much talk about the 'divine spark' in every human being, and the fostering of cosy, chatty relationships with the Lord. Perhaps the trend of events is now making it possible for us to listen more patiently to a theology that confronts us with a truly holy God and takes seriously the predicament of the human race in its frustrations, agony, and near despair.

The root words in Paul's thinking about God are all derivatives of what we call 'right'. Words that come out very differently in English are all associated with this basic root. 'Righteousness', 'justice', 'justification' – all have to do with what is right and the central question of how we can be 'right with God'. Modern translations have tried to bring this out by modifying the direct translation of certain Greek words. For instance, when Paul says of the Gospel that 'therein is the righteousness of God revealed' (Romans 1:17, KJV) the King James version has a straightforward translation of the Greek. But the meaning is brought out for us today when the new translation has: 'The Gospel reveals how God puts men right with himself.' Similarly the King James version has familiarized millions with the declaration: 'A man is not justified by the works of the law, but by the faith of Jesus Christ', whereas we can now read in words that carry the thought much more clearly to our ears: 'A man is put right with God only through faith in Jesus Christ, never by doing what the Law requires.'

The word 'righteousness' is retained in some places in the new translation, but it is normally avoided since to our ears it carries overtones of 'self-righteous', or 'over-righteous'. We should think of Paul as possessed by the thought of God's burning goodness, and absolute justice, and how we human beings can possibly be related to this perfect and demanding 'rightness'. It is when he is dealing with this subject (it is the major theme of Galatians as well as Romans) that Paul ceases to be the mystic and becomes the intellectual, the theologian, the arguer, the persuader. It is his dealing with this subject that has given him the reputation of a system-builder, a dogmatist, a wrestler with abstruse ideas, or even a juggler with words and symbols. We cannot over-estimate the importance for Paul of what has been called his doctrine of 'justification by faith', but as we try to get at what he really means we shall see that for him this was no battle of words, no theoretical hobby-horse he liked to ride, but literally a matter of life and death. And who are we to say that the question of how people like us can be set 'right with God' is any less urgent than it was to him?

What is not easy for us to enter into is Paul's formid-able background in the Law as contained in the Old Testament books and annotated and expounded by generations of scribes. It is hard to talk about what this Law meant in a few moments without the risk of over-simplification and caricature. Briefly it could be said that in the Mosaic Law, with its moral and ritual de-mands, there was spelled out what being right with God means in practice. Although Paul came to believe that no amount of determination to obey every jot and tittle of the Law could really set us right with God, he never wavered in his belief that it reflected the righteous-ness of God. 'We know that the Law is good, if it is used as it should be used' (1 Timothy 1:8). 'The Law was in charge of us until Christ came, so that we might be put right with God through faith' (Galatians 3:24). Paul's own experience as a Pharisee explained the vehemence with which he kept referring to what the Law could and could not do. Being right with God had meant for him a desperate struggle to keep every item in the moral and ritual Law in the traditions of Judaism. 'So far as keeping the Jewish Law is concerned, I was a Pharisee,' he writes (Philippians 3:5) '. . . So far as a man can be righteous by obeying the commands of the Law, I was without fault.'

If any should feel that this obsession of Paul with the Law makes his writings on this theme of interest only to the religious historian, and that therefore we cannot expect much enlightenment from such passages in the letters, it would not take long to demonstrate that

legalistic religion is still with us. We don't need to delve
into the rigorist views of some of Paul's Jewish contemporaries to understand his continual references to
the contrast between Law and grace. Indeed, it would be
presumptuous for a Christian to assume that the Judaism
of his day or ours had no conception of the grace and
mercy of God, and was totally dominated by the thought
of earning God's favour by obedience to the Law. One
has only to read Psalm 119 to discover that a devout
Jew found joy and a deep sense of God's mercy in the
Law. 'I have longed for thy salvation, O Lord; and thy
law is my delight.' 'Thy righteousness is an everlasting
righteousness, and thy law is the truth.' 'Unless thy law
had been my delight, I should then have perished in
mine affliction.' Whoever wrote this psalm was no
miserable slave to a religion of commandments and
ceremonies. On the other hand in every age Christians
have tended to slip into this very legalism that Paul is
fighting. Whenever you hear remarks like: 'I don't
worry about creeds: my religion is the Sermon on the
Mount' or 'I've tried to live a decent life and help others –
isn't that all the religion I need?' or 'I've always sup-
ported the Church so I reckon God will take care of me'
or 'On the whole I think I've earned my way to heaven',
you're listening to the very legalism that Paul was shouting out in almost every letter. And it is remarkable how
in every century the tendency in the Church to transform
the Gospel into a burden to be borne, into a system of
rewards and punishments, has been resisted and transformed by a revival of the insights of the apostle. That is
why 'justification by faith' became the motto of the
Reformers.

The corollary to Paul's theme of 'the righteousness of
God' (which with him is not a static notion of sheer moral
perfection, but a dynamic phrase suggesting a yearning
to communicate this 'rightness' to men) is, of course, his
concept of sin. Paul is often accused of being obsessed
by human sins, and is pictured as a churlish preacher
eager to condemn every moral lapse in the members of
his churches. In fact, he has surprisingly little to say
about *sins* as specific acts, but a great deal to say about
sin as a power to be reckoned with in the human heart.

It is mostly in his letter to the Romans that he deals with sin as the fatal flaw in human nature that makes necessary our reconciliation with God, our being 'set right', forgiven, but every letter has something to say about the sin from which we need to be delivered. We need to understand that sin is for him something infinitely more than an occasional lapse on the part of a man or woman who is otherwise in happy communion with God. It is, as our Lord says in the Fourth Gospel, a slavery of the soul (John 8:34). Paul makes more than one attempt to explain the origin of sin – it is the result of the basic disobedience of Adam; it is the expression of the lower side of human nature (what he calls 'the flesh' – by which he does not mean the body); it is a captivity by demonic forces beyond man's control – but he is more concerned about finding the answer to its power. And that he proclaims in his interpretation of the Good News as being set right, and made right, by the grace of God in Christ received by faith.

If this sounds a little complicated that shows our need to think now of these two absolutely dominant words in Paul's letters – grace and faith.

The little word 'grace' occurs, by my count, ninety times in the letters of Paul. This time we needn't worry at all about questions of translations. The Greek word *charis* can, as far as I know, be translated no other way. It is probably the most important single word in all Paul's writings – or even in the entire New Testament. No one could really hear the Good News according to Paul without having at least a glimpse of the wealth of meaning he pours into this word.

Let me suggest at this point that there is a limit to what any commentary, dictionary, or lexicon can do in the way of explaining the meaning of one word by the use of others. If we are ready to be convinced, as Paul was, that something utterly and tremendously new had appeared with the life, death, and resurrection of Jesus Christ, we should be prepared to concede to him, and the other New Testament writers, the right to use an untranslatable word – untranslatable, that is, into any other concepts or ideas. There was a Hebrew word, which the King James version of the Old Testament translates 'grace', or 'favour', ('finding grace in thy sight' may sound familiar); and there was this Greek word in everyday speech which was used to denote either charm, or loveliness, (as in our use of 'graceful') or goodwill and gratitude in human relationships. When Paul and his Christian friends used this word much of its Old Testament meaning, and some of the contemporary pagan, must have attached to it, but they poured into it the whole content of the Good News. In other words, it expressed for them God's miraculous answer to the burning question of how we can get right with him – and that answer was his gift of Jesus Christ. What Paul is saying in a hundred ways in his letters can be summed up in one phrase: 'The grace of our Lord Jesus Christ', and in one sentence: 'It is by God's grace that you have been saved.'

If grace cannot be translated it can be experienced, and it can, in a thousand ways, be pictured or described. For Paul it is supremely the answer to the question of getting right with God. Behind every line of these letters is a man who, after the most intense, even heartbreaking efforts, to win God's favour by a meticulous observance of the Law, suddenly found himself at the receiving end of an overwhelming divine love and knew that he was accepted for no other reason than that love which for him was focused on the person of Jesus Christ. Grace then became for him the realization of the great words of John's Gospel that 'God loved the world so much that he gave his only Son, so that everyone who believes in him may not die but have eternal life.' Whatever Paul says about grace springs, not from the mind of a scholar elaborating a new doctrine, but from the heartbeat of a man whose life had been transformed by an encounter with the living Christ. That is why we don't find any formal definitions of grace in the letters but rather a series of eruptions of joy and gratitude. The pagan might well begin a letter with this very word: 'Charis (grace), be to you', but when Paul set down the word his thoughts raced off to its intense and enlivening Christian meaning: 'May God our Father and the Lord Jesus Christ give you grace and peace.' (Romans 1:7) Grace is the accept-ance and forgiveness that he devoutly wished for all to whom he wrote, and peace the resultant sense of being 'right with God'. It's as if we were to write the formal words 'Dear John' and then pour into the adjective all that it means to discover that we truly are dear in God's sight. (Liturgical revisers who want to abolish the old phrase 'Dearly beloved' from, for instance, the marriage service might remember that the intention is to proclaim the Good News that all who hear are indeed beloved of God, and not to claim some false familiarity with the assembled guests.)

Whenever Paul speaks of grace he means a deeply personal experience of God. The Church over the years with its incurable habit of systematizing and regulating the truths of the Gospel has often given the impression that grace is a kind of holy oil, originally supplied by her Lord, and now dispensed to the needy through the proper channels. Thus the expression the 'means of grace' can come to mean something like the pipelines by which this oil reaches the faithful. In Paul's thinking the 'means of grace' would be much more like the simple things that keep a friendship in repair, such as sharing experiences, being together, writing to each other, and mutual unburdening; or like those that hold a family together in common acceptance and love, like eating together, talking things over, observing birthdays and festivals, being drawn closer through common joys and sorrows. We come near to Paul's so-called 'doctrine of grace' when we remember that a friendship is not formed or kept by some mutual agreement to abide by certain rules, nor is a happy family one that is governed by law and in which children have to earn their parents' love by strict obedience. Think personally with Paul, and you will understand more clearly what he is saying about grace.

Look at some of the things he says. Speaking of his call to be an apostle, having seen the risen Christ, he breaks off to confess that he has not deserved such a gift: 'But by God's grace I am what I am, and the grace that he gave me was not without effect.' He goes on to speak of his hard work as an apostle but cannot help adding immediately: 'it was not really my own doing, but God's grace working with me.' (1 Corinthians 15:10) In his moving words about his 'thorn in the flesh' he tells us that when, in spite of his fervent prayers, the thorn was not removed he heard the Lord's answer: 'My grace is all you need; for my power is strongest when you are weak.' He tells us more than once what it is that keeps him going as he ministers to these little churches and constantly moves on to new and dangerous territory. 'God, in his grace, has given me this work to do for your good' (Ephesians 3:2). 'Our relations with you,' he writes to the recalcitrant Corinthians, 'have been ruled by God-given frankness and sincerity, by the power of God's grace, and not by human wisdom' (2 Corinthians 1:12). It is no wonder that he keeps on commending these new Christians to the same sustaining grace – this accepting and fortifying knowledge of God's personal presence. 'As for you, my son, be strong through the grace that is ours in union with Christ Jesus' (2 Timothy 2:1).

It is when we have caught this note of intimate communion with Christ, of joyful acceptance by God, of the freedom of the Spirit within, that we shall understand why he at times becomes almost fierce in the defence of this Good News. The polemics of the letter to the Galatians are occasioned by the insistence of some Jewish Christians that Gentiles must be circumcised and enjoined to keep the Law. He detected in this apparently reasonable requirement a fatal reversion to the idea that we win God's favour by our religious observance and moral rectitude. So he called this trend a 'falling from grace'. The importance of the Galatian letter for us is not as an ancient document from some distant controversy but as an ever-essential reminder that we cannot have it both ways. We cannot at the same time believe that our salvation is a pure gift of God's grace and try still to earn it by our efforts. You cannot work in any church today, or attend any ecclesiastical conference, without learning that the Galatian heresy is not dead. How many of us really know what it is to live by grace – humbly throwing ourselves day by day on the mercy of God, accepting what comes to us with thanksgiving, and never for one moment congratulating ourselves on our moral standards or spiritual insights?

Once again we shall realize how closely Paul followed

the teaching of Jesus on this subject. For the best illustrations of what he is telling us about grace are to be found in the Gospels. There are the parables of the Prodigal Son, the Labourers in the Vineyard, and the Pharisee and the Publican at prayer. (You will remember the Lord's words about the man who made no claim but pleaded: 'God, have pity on me, a sinner!' 'I tell you this man, and not the other, was in the right with God when he went home.') And there are the many references to God's acceptance of the sinful, the desolate, the outcast, coupled with his rejection of the proud, the self-righteous, and the self-justifiers.

If 'grace' is the most important word of all in Paul's vocabulary very close to it is 'faith'. We put grace first only because it speaks of the primacy of God's action in our salvation. This is an important point as we come to consider what Paul means by faith. For faith has often been exalted as the single all-sufficing principle for the Christian life. 'By faith alone' has been said, for instance, to be the battle-cry of the Reformers, and today whenever people speak about religion it is usually in terms of faith. The difference between a religious person and an irreligious is said to be that the one has faith while the other hasn't. Whereas the Reformers always meant specific faith in Christ as Lord and Saviour, the modern man or woman tends to speak of faith as an end in itself. It doesn't seem to matter whom we have faith in, or what the content of our faith may be. Just as we were told that 'there is nothing to fear but fear itself', so others seem to be telling us: 'There is nothing to have faith in but faith itself.'

For Paul faith is nothing other than our response to the grace of God in Christ. 'For it is by God's gift that you have been saved' is not the entire sentence that Paul wrote. 'It is by God's grace that you have been saved, *through faith*.' It is, therefore, a personal response to a personal gift. This is the best place to begin understanding Paul's use of the word faith – as the kind of trust that we put in one who offers us his friendship. The simpler the illustration the better. If I have offended someone and feel I cannot be forgiven, and if that person comes and offers me not only forgiveness but friendship, I have the option of rejecting the approach, or trusting him completely and entering into a new and restored relationship. That is faith, as Paul normally uses the word. It is a personal trust in the God whom Jesus Christ reveals.

When Paul writes to the Galatians about their Christian experience, he puts the question this way: 'When God gives you the Spirit and works miracles among you, does he do it because you do what the Law requires, or because you hear and believe the Gospel?' This hearing and believing the Good News is what for him constitutes this new relationship of friendship and 'rightness with God'. It is more than a matter of listening to a proposition about what God has done and assenting to its truth. This 'hearing' is something alive and personal, and the 'hearing of faith' is what to this day makes a man or woman a Christian. Writing to the Romans Paul describes what we would call evangelism in terms of this receptive hearing of the Good News. He uses a text from the Old Testament, as he often does, to illuminate the point. 'As the scripture says, "Everyone who calls on the name of the Lord will be saved" ', then he goes on: 'But how can they call to him, if they have not believed? And how can they believe, if they have not heard the message? And how can they hear, if the message is not proclaimed? And how can the message be proclaimed, if the messengers are not sent out?' These words give us an insight into the way Paul conceived the Christian mission, how the message was declared, and what he expected to happen. There is no attempt to describe exactly how a man or woman comes to make this response of faith. When Christ is declared as the bearer of the grace of God, the liberator from sin and death, the true Lord of our lives, faith is awakened and the new life is born.

It is clear then that the Good News is not a proclamation that through grace all are automatically saved. Whatever may be drawn from the New Testament as to the ultimate destiny of the whole human race the apostles unanimously insisted that our entering into the family of God depends on our response of faith. Lest any should begin to boast of their faith as an achievement that earns them their reward Paul is careful to speak of faith as a gift of the Spirit. It is his insistence on the fact that we owe our salvation entirely to God that leads him into the difficult and dangerous waters of 'election', and 'predestination'. (The latter doctrine was not, as many seem to think, the invention of John Calvin but is adumbrated in both Old and New Testaments, and appears in some form in every major theologian from Augustine to Aquinas to Barth.) We have here a paradox for our thinking but a truth that Christian experience bears out. We know, as all the New Testament writers knew, that we have the choice to respond to the Good News or not – and the choice is free. But we also know the voice that says from inside the Christian experience: 'You did not choose me; I chose you.' By the grace of God, and not by my wonderful capacity for faith, I am what I am.

The letters instruct all Christians that the way of discipleship is lit up by this inner faith in Christ which gives us a different perspective on life from that of the unbelieving world, and that by faith we are enabled to grow and mature even while the physical body is running down. In a striking passage we read: 'The scripture says, "I spoke because I believed." In the same spirit of faith, we also speak because we believe. For we know that God, who raised the Lord Jesus to life, will also raise us up with Jesus and bring us, together with you, into his presence. All this is for your sake; and as God's grace reaches more and more people, they will offer more prayers of thanksgiving, to the glory of God. For this reason we never become discouraged. Even though our physical being is gradually decaying, yet our spiritual being is renewed day after day . . . For we fix our attention, not on things that are seen, but on things that are unseen. What can be seen lasts only for a time; but what cannot be seen lasts forever' (2 Corinthians 4:13-18). He sums it all up by saying: 'For our life is a matter of faith, not of sight.' (2 Corinthians 5:7)

Faith then is not only the means by which we first accept the Good News but the principle by which a Christian lives. In a very personal note to Philemon he writes: 'Every time I pray, brother Philemon, I mention you and give thanks to my God. For I hear of your love for all God's people and the faith you have in the Lord

Jesus. My prayer is that our fellowship with you as believers will bring about a deeper understanding of every blessing which we have in our life in Christ.' To the Thessalonian church he writes: 'We must thank God at all times for you, brothers. It is right for us to do so, because your faith is growing so much as the love each of you has for the others is becoming greater . . . We boast about the way you continue to endure and believe' (2 Thessalonians 1:3, 4). To the Ephesian church he sends the beautiful prayer that 'Christ will make his home in your hearts, through faith' (Ephesians 3:17). His personal confession is: 'This life that I live now, I live by faith in the Son of God, who loved me and gave his life for me.'

The tenor of these passages, and there are many others, is such that we can be sure that for Paul, as for Jesus, faith was primarily trust in a person and not assent to a proposition. In no letter does Paul either define faith by some formula or suggest that it consists in deciding to adhere to specific propositions about God, Christ, and the Spirit. In the later letters, especially in the pastoral epistles that are usually believed to have been at least edited by a later hand, there are the beginnings of the Church's use of 'the faith' to indicate the content of the Good News. Timothy is called: 'my true son in the faith' (1 Timothy 1:2) and church officers are warned that 'they should hold to the revealed truth of the faith with a clear conscience' (1 Timothy 3:9). In the same way we find in his parting testimony the expression: 'I have kept the faith.' (2 Timothy 4:7) From this use of the word 'faith', meaning the content of the Christian message, there developed the notion that faith is chiefly to be identified with holding correct doctrines, so that eventually the Athanasian Creed could preface its astonishingly complex theological propositions with the words: 'Which faith except everyone keep whole and undefiled without doubt he shall perish everlastingly.'

Faith, of course, has a content, and there must be some expression of the truths we believe and the person in whom we trust. Paul, in these letters, spends no time in commending faith as a healthful psychological exercise. But for him it is never a formal adherence to a doctrine.

It is a living relationship to God through Jesus Christ. It is not a matter of a temperamental disposition to believe or even of a persuasion of the mind. It is the breath of life. It is our daily Yes to the God of grace. It is being led by the Spirit of God (Romans 8:14). It is the persuasion of our entire being that 'there is nothing in all creation that will ever be able to separate us from the love of God which is ours through Christ Jesus our Lord' (Romans 8:39).

It might be argued that there are other key words essential to the understanding of his Gospel – 'love', for instance, or 'calling', or 'hope', or 'the Spirit'. Each of these has great importance if we are to grasp his exposition of the Good News. But the ones we have reviewed seem to me so typical of the man who wrote these letters, so essential for our sympathetic hearing of them today, that they call for special consideration. It is surprising what a difference it can make when reading an author from an age far removed from ours if we give to some of his favourite words something of the colour, the weight, and the flavour that they had for him.

4. UNDERSTANDING HIS CONTROVERSIES

A certain proportion of the correspondence of one who holds any kind of public position is bound to be controversial. Positions have to be defended, accusations answered, explanations offered, supporters encouraged, opponents exposed and, if you like, the disaffected made affected and the disgruntled made gruntled. Politicians must labour under this necessity more than anyone else but the clergy are not exempt. From the very beginning the Christian Church had both its external and internal controversies which are reflected throughout the New Testament writings. Though Jesus himself left no correspondence, and may not have had any, it is interesting that on the only occasion on which it is recorded that he wrote (it may have been a mere doodle in the dust) he was in controversy with religious leaders who wanted to trap him into either condemning or excusing a woman taken in adultery (John 8:1-10). The book of the Acts tells us of the young Church's verbal battle with both Hebrew tradition and pagan culture and superstition, and frankly records disturbances within the Church such as the appeal to the Council of Jerusalem for a ruling on the question of the adherence of Gentile converts to the Jewish Law (Acts 15) and personal disputes such as that between Paul and Barnabas over the behaviour of John Mark (Acts 15:36-9). 'They had a sharp argument between them,' notes Luke drily.

The period after the recognition of Christianity as the favoured religion of the Roman Empire was marked by tremendous controversy about matters of doctrine and Church order, and letters flew from city to city, and church to church, filled with argument, denunciation, exposition, and refutation. From the Reformation to the present day, great crises within the Church have always been marked by vigorous correspondence among Church leaders, and the issuing of declarations, proclamations, and counter-proclamations. We may deplore the vehemence and lack of charity in much of this controversy, but what live movement of the human spirit was ever launched, what new truths ever came to be accepted, without verbal sparks flying and much epistolary heat being generated? The Church has always been at its most vigorous in society when genuine theological differences were being freely aired. Not every example of rough exchange of letters (between, for example, Augustine and Pelagius, Luther, Calvin, and Zwingli, Barth, and Brunner) can be written off as symptoms of that dreaded disease known as *odium theologicum*. You might even say that a lack of such altercation indicates a lethargic Church where no one really cares enough about any doctrine to get mad.

All this should be kept in mind when we turn to the controversial aspect of Paul's letters. We must realize that this was the most critical period in the Church's history. Not only had these first Christians to find a way of formulating the new truths in which they had come to believe and to be on their guard against any modifications of the content of the Good News that would either make it cease to be 'new' or make it just another 'mystery cult', but they had to make decisions that would determine the entire future direction of the Church. The basic controversy, as we have seen, centred on the attitude to be adopted towards the Gentile converts – whether or not they were to be required to be subject to the Jewish Law and all that it entailed. It is this question that hovers over a lot of Paul's writing and accounts for some of his most vigorous, and to many today incomprehensible, passages of argument and rebuttal. Other controversies that surface in his correspondence have to do with morals, with Church behaviour, with the employment of 'spiritual gifts', and with the intrusion into the churches of philosophies and practices that seemed destructive of Christian truth.

We may feel like remarking that there is nothing so dead as a dead controversy and that we would find the going less rough when reading these epistles if we could skip all the passages that echo the sound of 'old, unhappy, far-off things, and battles long ago'. It may well be that in Paul's letters, as in other parts of the Bible, there are some matters that have little interest for us today (though the Bible has a curious way of coming alive again in each generation at the very points where a previous generation had closed its eyes), but when we go on to examine the major themes that arouse the apostle, I believe we shall find that they touch on questions that are basic to the understanding of the Gospel in any age, and often quite dramatically in ours. The trouble for the average reader is that a lack of knowledge of the original cause of dispute often obscures what is being said about matters that concern us, both individually and as a Church, in the twentieth century. It is, of course, perfectly possible to read these letters as they stand with a minimal knowledge of the historical background. Millions have done so – and heard the Word of God in them; but some information about the controversies that rumbled through them can enable us at points to hear that Word more clearly, and certainly will add to the interest they arouse. This little book can do no more than sketch the various situations that stimulated Paul to dispatch these letters to specific churches or people at a specific time, and even a vastly more scholarly work would have to admit that, in some cases, we still do not have enough material to perceive exactly what the controversy was about.

We could begin with what is perhaps the best known controversy and the most polemic of the letters – the Epistle to the Galatians. Our study of the meaning of the words 'grace', 'Law', 'righteousness', and 'justification', has already introduced the critical decision that was being forced upon the churches. The book of the Acts indicates that, with Peter's experience in a Roman officers' mess (Acts 10) and the response of the non-Jewish world to the preaching of the first evangelists who left Jerusalem, it had been joyfully agreed that the Good News was to be shared with the Gentiles. The real issue then emerged: were these Gentiles to be required to keep the Jewish Law – which meant, in short, must they be not only baptized into Christ, but circumcised 'into the Law'. Nothing is more wearisome and apparently meaningless to the average modern congregation than to listen to Paul's apparent obsession with this matter of circumcision, a word that occurs over forty times in his correspondence. (I have often found myself obliged to avoid a passage for public reading that contained the very verse I wanted as a text for a sermon simply because that verse was embedded in a maze of references to circumcision. 'Freedom is what we have – Christ has set us free! Stand, then, as free men, and do not allow yourselves to become slaves again.' These magnificent words are followed immediately by such a tirade about circumcision as would cause the uninstructed modern WASP to switch off.)

For Paul this particular Jewish rite had enormous significance at this very point. He was not rejecting his own Jewish background in any way, or scoffing at this sign of the Covenant God had made with his chosen people. He was simply pouncing on the very action – forcing a Gentile convert to be circumcised – that symbolized a refusal to accept the Good News that we are saved by grace through faith in Jesus Christ. That was the message that had brought him freedom and he had seen it bring such freedom to the Gentiles in Galatia when he preached it to them. What infuriated him and makes this letter sound the harshest and most violent of them all was the fact that, almost as soon as he had left this church to go on with his missionary journeys, a group of Jewish Christians (probably from Jerusalem) had arrived and started at once to undermine his work by telling the new converts that the Good News they had joyfully received was quite inadequate and had to be supplemented by reception into the Jewish religion through circumcision. 'We're OK,' they said in effect, 'but you're not OK – until you accept the obligations of the Law.' 'These people,' says Paul, who can hardly contain himself when referring to their activities, 'had slipped in as spies, to find out about the freedom we have through our union with Christ Jesus' (Galatians 2:4).

Quite apart from the fact that Paul was here fighting the battle whose outcome made possible the spread of Christianity across the entire world and the expansion of the Church into every community, he is also warning us of the perennial efforts of misguided Christians to add to the simple Good News some set of legalistic requirements. In our own times we have seen mission work by devoted preachers infiltrated by some group who try to persuade the converts that they have been misled and that the true Gospel involves accepting their particular tenets about belief and behaviour. The divisive and deluding work of extremists with a special emphasis or special requirements can be paralleled in almost every sector of the great mission field that is our world today.

Paul felt so strongly about this that he declares he had a show-down on the subject with no less a person than Peter himself. Peter did not belong to this party of 'Judaizers', but he was anxious not to offend them. So on one occasion in the city of Antioch, after mingling freely with the Gentile Christians, he thought it politic to withdraw from them when some of these 'Judaizers' arrived and would not eat with them any more. Paul was incensed by what seemed to him cowardice on Peter's part. 'I opposed him in public,' he writes, 'because he was clearly wrong' (Galatians 2:11). This is the kind of situation that constantly arises in the Church and we can recognize it today. A and B are both agreed that C's views are wrong. But while A wants a show-down, B is willing to compromise for the sake of peace. This apostolic clash could be a good starting-point for a discussion on Christian strategy and tactics today.

Outside the letters to Rome and Galatia we do not hear too much of this 'Judaizing' controversy, but Paul was never long away from equally disturbing and vigorous contention in the churches he had founded. The most strife-ridden church of all seems to have been the one in Corinth. The two letters that have come down to us are among the most precious of all Christian documents. They contain not only the superb hymn to Christian love (1 Corinthians 13), but also the majestic argument concerning the Resurrection with its triumphant climax – 'Where, Death, is your victory? Where, Death, is your power to hurt? . . . But thanks be to God who gives us the victory through our Lord Jesus Christ!'

(1 Corinthians 15:55, 57) – and the powerful description
of the 'gifts of the Spirit' within the membership of the
Body of Christ, the words of institution that are embodied
in our service of Holy Communion, the moving passage
about the growth of our 'spiritual being' while we look
at the things that are not seen, and a great number of
sentences that have been the text for thousands of
sermons. Yet, we should notice that every one of these
classic passages springs out of a specific situation that
has been brought to his attention. We ought never to
think of Paul as composing any of these inspired passages
in the isolation of a spiritual ivory tower for the edification of posterity. They flowed from his pen as he addressed himself to the problems and controversies of
churches like ours today.

We are accustomed to the solemn words that give us
the warrant for the celebration of the sacrament of the
Lord's Supper: 'I have received of the Lord that which
also I delivered unto you, that the Lord Jesus the same
night in which he was betrayed took bread . . .' (1
Corinthians 11:23, KJV) What we may have forgotten
is that these words are preceded by a slashing attack on
the appalling disorder into which the Corinthian
Christians had allowed the sacrament to lapse. Apparently it had become a kind of orgy in which everyone
grabbed his own supplies regardless of his neighbour's
needs. 'When you meet together as a group,' he writes,
'you do not come to eat the Lord's Supper. For as you
eat, each one goes ahead with his own meal, so that
some are hungry while others get drunk. Don't you have
your own homes in which to eat and drink? Or would
you rather despise the church of God and put to shame
the people who are in need? What do you expect me to
say to you about this? Should I praise you? Of course
I do not praise you!' (1 Corinthians 11:20-2) These
flaming words of indignation come *immediately* before
the solemn words on the institution of the Lord's Supper.

The rhapsody about Christian love which has been
enthroned in the literature of the world arose out of an
attempt by Paul to settle quite acrimonious disputes
about which Christian has the better gift of the Spirit.
He has had to stress the fact that the Church contains

people of very varied gifts. 'Christ is like a single body, which has many parts; it is still one body, even though it is made up of different parts' (1 Corinthians 12:12). These Corinthians were evidently torn apart by the rival claims of those who were preachers, teachers, healers, counsellors, speakers in 'tongues', and social workers.

Paul lists the different gifts, and points out that no one can have them all. Then he quietly goes on to say: 'Best of all, however, is the following way', and proceeds to commend love as the all-inclusive, all-important gift of the Holy Spirit. We are true to Paul's thinking when, instead of paying lip-service to a beautiful passage, we relate it, as he did, to the question of foolish rivalries in the service of the Church.

Similarly we can readily detect in his great exposition of the doctrine of the Resurrection the echoes of the questions that had risen in the Corinthian church. He even quotes the people he is refuting. 'How can some of you say that the dead will not be raised to life?' (1 Corinthians 15:12) 'Someone will ask, "How can the dead be raised to life? What kind of body will they have?"' (v. 35) Such questions are exactly those that we hear today. Another reference (v. 29) to his troublemakers in Corinth is more obscure to us. 'Now, what of those people who are baptized for the dead? What do they hope to accomplish?' Yet, it is not unknown today for theories and practices to arise that have to do with the salvation of our ancestors. What matters is that we read Paul's exposition with the understanding that he is not composing a final statement about the Christian doctrine of the Resurrection but answering real questions from real people.

One of the most acute questions for the early Church lies behind a great deal of what he writes both to the Corinthians and to other churches. And it is a very live question in our churches today. It has to do with his doctrine of salvation by grace through faith. When the 'Judaizers' protested that this doctrine, by teaching young converts that they were not saved by keeping the Law of God, encouraged them to adopt a policy of 'anything goes' in the Christian life, they had a point. For it seems clear that quite a number of these Christians in Corinth were arguing that since they lived by grace and not by law, they could freely indulge in all kinds of licentious conduct that was sternly forbidden in the Old Testament. You can imagine how upset Paul would be by this caricature of his doctrine – and yet how difficult it was to show that his assault on the Law as a means of salvation was intended to produce a higher, and not a lower, level of morality. There is nothing more infuriating than to find your deepest belief so twisted by your own supporters that your opponents can gleefully say: 'I told you so.'

Paul quotes the arguments of these misguided Christians. 'What shall we say, then?' he asks. 'That we should continue to live in sin so that God's grace will increase?' (Romans 6:1) Tell somebody that he is saved by grace, and not through any merit of his own, and he may well be tempted to say: 'If God's grace is so marvellous then the more blatantly I sin the more grace is needed and the more glory to God.' Sounds logical, doesn't it? Again he quotes from his Corinthian Christians: 'Someone will say, "I am allowed to do anything."' (1 Corinthians 6:12) This seems to have been a current phrase at the time – not unlike, even in its intention and results, these two items of current jargon – 'permissiveness' and 'situational ethics'. 'All things are lawful' is the familiar translation. He quotes it again (1 Corinthians 10:23) – 'we are allowed to do anything so they say.' 'All things are lawful.'

This perversion of the apostle's teaching about grace has a technical name as formidable as the error – antinomianism. And antinomianism is the ghost that has shadowed the teaching of salvation by grace through the centuries. It is precisely this misreading of the essential Gospel which Paul is attacking that has caused shock waves in the Church in recent years. In reaction to the perversion of legalism which tended to dominate certain sections of the Church in the first half of this century, there has been a great swing in some quarters to the philosophy of 'anything goes'. There are few eccentricities of conduct, or repudiations of traditional Christian morality, which will not be hailed today somewhere as an expression of Christian love, and almost no kind of behaviour that will not be defended as an 'alternative life-style'.

Note how Paul deals with this misinterpretation of his Gospel. Generally speaking, he relies on the argument that the compulsion of grace is such that, if we have genuinely received it, we cannot even conceive that we have been given a licence to sin. So he answers the Roman Christians' question about exalting grace by sinning all the more with a sharp: 'Certainly not!' 'God forbid!' (KJV) The Greek expression is a vigorous negative which he is inclined to use whenever he finds his teaching being misapplied. He has not time for any doctrine of what Dietrich Bonhoeffer called 'cheap grace'. That we owe our salvation entirely to the grace of God and not to our own virtue by no means implies that we can break the law of God freely and with impunity. There is a greater constraint in living by the love of Christ than the Law could ever exert, in Paul's experience – and in ours.

He answers the slogan 'I am allowed to do anything' three times. The first time he simply says, 'Yes; but not everything is good for you,' – a blunt answer every sensible Christian can appreciate. Then he makes a second stab at an answer. 'I could say, "I am allowed to do anything," but I am not going to let anything make a slave of me.' That is a reply to ponder. The third time he quotes 'we are allowed to do everything,' he not only repeats that 'not everything is good' but adds 'but not everything is helpful.' Clearly he is concerned to warn all Christians about the dangerous possibilities of the popular slogan.

These letters, like the one to the Romans, show real concern about the conscience of the Christian as he mixes with the pagan world. Now that the western world has broken loose from the moorings of Christendom, and the moral assumptions of the average citizen are no longer necessarily those of the believing Christian, we find ourselves in a position to understand the tensions of the Christian conscience much better than our fore-fathers. Paul found himself called to advise on all kinds of questions, from what seem the most trivial to matters that have troubled Christians in every age – such as the conflicting loyalties to Church and state.

Paul seems to have followed the practice of other Christian leaders of the time in counselling Christians to be loyal subjects of the state in all matters that did not compromise the ultimate Christian loyalties. His much quoted and much disputed advice to the Romans that 'Everyone must obey the state authorities; because no authority exists without God's permission, and the existing authorities have been put there by God' (Romans 13:1) is in line with what is said in the First Epistle of Peter: 'Submit yourselves, for the Lord's sake, to every human authority; to the Emperor, who is the supreme authority, and to the governors, who have been sent by him to punish the evildoers and praise those who do good.' At this time in the Church's story the emphasis seems to have been on obedience to the civil authorities unless they demanded the kind of allegiance, even worship, that no Christian can give. There is no evidence in these letters that there was much dispute about this, and the apostles seem to have been anxious that Christians should not get into trouble for the wrong reasons.

We can, however, detect in Paul's correspondence signs of the strains put upon Christians in their daily contact with the pagan world. In a vivid passage in First Corinthians he raises the question of Christians bringing their disputes before a pagan court. Although he accepts and respects the legal system under which they live, he is deeply troubled by the thought that Christians should be unable to settle their differences in the spirit of the Gospel. 'If one of you has a dispute with a brother, how dare he go before heathen judges, instead of letting God's people settle the matter?' (1 Corinthians 6:1) We get a glimpse of how close-knit he felt a church community should be, and how horrified he was by the thought of Christians having to appeal to a pagan court. 'Shame on you! Surely there is at least one wise man in your fellowship who can settle a dispute between the brothers. Instead, one brother goes to court against another, and lets unbelievers judge the case!' (6:5, 6) He advocates the practice of what we would call the 'ethics of Jesus' within the fellowship, saying that it would be better to be victimized than to haul a brother before the pagan court. That matters should even come to this pass within the fellowship distresses him greatly. 'The very fact that you have legal disputes among yourselves shows that you have failed completely. Would it not be better for you to be wronged? Would it not be better for you to be robbed?' The thought that such things were happening within the Church then led him to denounce again the moral chaos caused by the antinomians. He lists idol-worshippers, adulterers, perverts, robbers, the greedy, drunkards, slanderers, and law-breakers, and insists that this kind of behaviour has no place in the new life to which they have been called. 'Some of you were like that. But you have been cleansed from sin; you have been dedicated to God; you have been put right with God through the name of the Lord Jesus Christ and by the Spirit of our God.' Paul clearly believed in what has been called 'the expulsive power of a new affection'.

Still, even if a Christian steered clear of the more obvious vices of the society around him, his conscience could be troubled by questions of contamination in his social contacts. It appears from the letters that Paul did not expect the Christians to refrain from all socializing with unbelievers, and that he did not have much sympathy for those who were always on the lookout for occasions to flaunt their delicate conscience before their pagan friends. 'If an unbeliever invites you to a meal and you decide to go, eat what is set before you without asking any questions because of conscience' (1 Corinthians 10:27). The kind of question he had in mind was: 'Is this meat I am being served part of an animal that may have been offered to an idol?' Paul's answer to this kind of question was always a healthy mixture of common sense and Christian charity. Idols are nothing, he argued, so what does it matter where your meat has come from? (1 Corinthians 8:4-6) 'Food,' he says, 'will not improve our relationship with God; we shall not lose anything if we do not eat, nor shall we gain anything if we do eat' (8:8). He does, however, suggest that if one's host makes it very clear that the meat has been part of idol worship (perhaps to tease his Christian guests?) it would be better to refrain for the sake of other Christians present who might have a very tender conscience. This is the argument about the 'weaker brother' which he used more than once. Christians who have reached the point of true freedom in the faith should respect the conscience of those who are still bound by all kinds of scruples. 'Be careful, however,' he writes, 'and do not let your freedom of action make those who are weak in the faith fall into sin.' There is much in such extracts from the letters that can be applied to the clash of conscience that often arises among Christians today.

The Ephesian letter again reveals Paul's concern about the infiltration of pagan habits into the Christian Church. His constant references to all kinds of vice may surprise those who have cherished an image of the first Christian churches as models of piety and puritan behaviour. Look at some of the things, for instance, that are said to the Ephesians whose church appears to have been highly regarded by the apostles. 'Do not live any longer like the heathen, whose thoughts are worthless, and whose minds are in the dark . . . They have lost all feeling of shame; they give themselves over to vice, and do all sorts of indecent things without restraint. That was not what you learned about Christ!' (Ephesians 4:17-20) He spells out enough specific vices to give us a rather startling picture of what was going on in some sections of the church. 'No more lying, then!' Also he speaks about anger, and even finds it necessary to say that 'the man who used to rob must stop robbing and start working' (4:28). It is a disconcerting picture of what can happen in a Christian church that he paints for us when he says: 'Get rid of all bitterness, passion, and anger. No more shouting or insults. No more hateful feelings of any sort' (4:31). If it is perhaps reassuring to us to know that the Church of the first century, the Church of the martyrs, had also its factions, its rows, its occasional rowdy congregational meetings, it is more important for us to listen to the apostolic admonitions: 'Use only helpful words', 'Do not make God's Holy Spirit sad', and, above all, 'Be kind and tender-hearted to one another, and forgive one another, as God has forgiven you in Christ.'

The letters, seen from this angle, are a powerful reminder of the perils of sub-Christian behaviour within the Church and of its antidote in the Spirit of Christ. Paul has no illusions that he is writing to islands of sainthood in a sinful world – at least, not in our definition of sainthood. Paul used the word 'saint' simply as we would use the word 'Christian' – a word he never employs. This is why Today's English Version has replaced the King James 'saints' with expressions like 'God's people'. But, in spite of many heartaches and tears, Paul never gave up on these struggling churches, and some of the most heartening and moving passages in his letters occur as he reminds them, and us, of the resources of the Spirit for those who are conscious of their failures to live as true Christians. 'I remember you in my prayers,' he writes to the Ephesians, 'and ask the God of our Lord Jesus Christ, the glorious Father, to give you the Spirit, who will make you wise and reveal God to you, so that you will know him. I ask that your minds may be opened to see his light, so that you will know what is the hope to which he has called you, how rich are the wonderful blessings he promises his people, and *how very great is his power at work in us who believe*' (Ephesians 1:16-19). 'We ask our God,' he writes to the Thessalonians, 'to make you worthy of the life he called you to live. May he, by his power, fulfil all your desire for goodness and complete your work of faith.' If in these letters we hear Paul as our preacher, we may not have realized how wonderfully we have Paul as our pastor.

What about Paul the theologian? We have seen how much time he takes to expound his doctrines of grace and faith, but there are also references in these letters to some of the theological controversies that were already disturbing Church members and were soon to blaze up and endanger the unity of the Church. We need not enter into a prolonged discussion of the nature of all the theologies, philosophies, and practices that the apostles found it necessary to combat. They became known as 'heresies' because of their divisive nature (the word means 'party-spirit'). Most of the heresies that subsequently rent the Church had to do with views of Christ which denied either his real divinity or his real humanity, but at the time these letters were written, the chief danger seemed to come from the trend of religious thought known as Gnosticism. Since this word is a modern coinage and is being bandied about again today, it might be useful to have this definition from Hastings' *Dictionary of the Bible*. 'The name Gnosticism is a modern term used to classify a wide variety of religious sects in existence from the first century of our era until at least the ninth. What they had in common was the belief that the world was made and controlled by hostile powers or angels, that the essence of true human nature was a divine element (spark, spirit) not created by these powers, and that a redeemer had descended from the highest heaven to awaken the divine element in those men who were capable of redemption; redemption was given in the reception of this knowledge (*gnosis*).'

Paul's thoroughly Hebrew conviction that God alone is the creator of the universe, and his equally thorough Christian conviction that redemption was wrought by Jesus Christ and realized in a personal relationship to him, made all such teaching obnoxious. It is in the letter to the Colossians that he seems to address himself most directly to ideas of this kind and a little knowledge of this background is useful for our understanding of the controversy he had with some members of that church.

Scholars have talked for years about the 'Colossian heresy' but no one has ever been able to define it exactly. It seems, from Paul's remarks, that some of the Christians in this church had succumbed to the Gnostic ideas about the world being created by evil powers, and so launches into one of the most exalted celebrations of the cosmic activity of Christ that has ever been penned. Starting with the incisive declaration that 'Christ is the visible likeness of the invisible God', he goes on to assert that as the eternal Son of God (what John would call the Word), he was responsible for all creation. 'For by him God created everything in heaven and on earth, the seen and the unseen things, including spiritual powers, lords, rulers, and authorities. God created the whole universe through him and for him' (Colossians 1:15, 16). Since the thought of spiritual powers, angelic and demonic, has surfaced again in our day, we can listen with profit again to this Good News of a Christ whose creative and redemptive power is supreme in the universe. This background explains the curious references in this letter to 'special visions' and 'the worship of angels' (2:18). He insists that knowledge (*gnosis*) for the Christian is simply our relationship to Christ, and that it is not an esoteric doctrine but an open secret. 'I have been made a servant of the church by God,' he writes, 'who gave me this task to perform for your good. It is the task of fully proclaiming his message, which is the secret he hid through all past ages from all mankind, but has now revealed to his people. God's plan is this: to make known his secret to his people, this rich and glorious secret which he had for all peoples. And the secret is this: Christ is in you, which means that you will share the glory of God' (1:25-7).

A brief mention should be made of a theological question that caused a great deal of commotion in the churches at this time. Any casual reader of the letters to the Thessalonians is bound to notice the emphasis on the return of Christ in glory. This is a topic that had a much deeper impact on the thinking and planning of the early Church than most of us can now imagine. Most of them lived and acted in the very real expectation that in their own lifetime the course of world history would be ended by the coming of Christ as judge. So vivid was this expectation that some Christians were afraid that their friends who had died would somehow be excluded from the great day of the Lord's return. This is why Paul writes: 'Brothers, we want you to know the truth about those who have died, so that you will not be sad, as are those who have no hope. We believe that Jesus died and rose again; so we believe that God will bring with Jesus those who have died believing in him. This is the Lord's teaching that we tell you: we who are alive on the day the Lord comes will not go ahead of those who have died' (1 Thessalonians 4:13-15). This thought of what has come to be known as the Second Coming (though neither Paul nor any other New Testament writer uses the expression) has to be kept in mind also when Paul urges his converts to be zealous and not to sit around waiting for the great day, and when we estimate the value of his remarks on marriage and procreation. It should be noted, too, that this lively image of the Second Coming does not dominate his later letters as it does this early correspondence with the Thessalonians.

These, then, are some of the controversies that were throbbing in the background as Paul wrote his famous letters, and it helps to know something about them. It will also be apparent that few of them are 'dead ducks' for the modern Christian. Yet, perhaps a footnote would now be in order concerning the controversies that Paul did *not* get into. We may feel like protesting as we read these letters that he seems to accept without question social conditions and practices that have been in the forefront of Christian protest in modern times. The most obvious of these is the theory and practice of slavery. The very moving little letter of Paul to his friend Philemon in which he pleads with him to receive back into his household a runaway slave named Onesimus, contains no hint that Paul found it wrong that one man should own another as his own personal property. The emphasis in the letter is on the appeal to Philemon to act freely as a Christian in forgiving the slave (who seems to have decamped with some of his master's money) and to welcome him as a brother. 'Now,' says Paul, 'he is not just a slave, but much more than a slave: he is a dear brother in Christ.'

In the same way we find Paul giving advice to both masters and slaves as to how they should conduct themselves. 'Masters,' he writes, 'be right and fair in the way you treat your slaves. Remember that you too have a Master in heaven.' 'Slaves, obey your human masters in all things, and do it not only when they are watching you, just to gain their approval, but do it with a sincere heart, because of your reverence for the Lord' (Colossians 4:1; 3:22). These examples show how the Word of God speaks to a certain 'given' in human society at a certain time, but contains enough explosive to shatter that 'given' when the Christian conscience draws the full consequences of the Good News in Christ. We must admit that it took about eighteen centuries for the full meaning of what Paul said to the Galatians 'there is no difference . . . between slaves and free men' (Galatians 3:28) to dawn on the Church, but when it did the results were dramatic. So it is happening with that other 'no difference' which he claims for those in union with Christ. 'There is no difference between men and women.' That Paul had not himself fully accepted the consequences of what he wrote is evident from many passages in his letters, although there are others which indicate that he had transcended the patriarchal traditions in which he was raised. We cannot expect Paul to have jumped over the boundaries of the age in which he lived, except in so far as the Spirit had given him new insight. The new insights were there, and the Word of God has broken out again and again from his writings to lead the Church into a fuller realization of the implications of the Good News he was proclaiming. So, as we read his letters today we are not being bored by the echoes of dead controversies, but being led to see how Christians must wrestle again and again with adulterations or perversions of the Gospel, and indeed discover new implications of the truth Paul grasped with which we have to wrestle in the Church today.

5. HIS ETHICS AND DOCTRINE OF THE CHURCH

An alert reader of Paul's letters will expect to find in them not only indications of what the first generation of Christians believed but also of how they behaved. For the Good News about Jesus Christ which they had accepted meant far more than a change of religious belief, new thoughts about God, new convictions about human destiny, and new forms of worship. The evidence is that the Christian community, even in its elementary stages, impressed and startled pagan contemporaries as a new way of life. The Good News was not only being accepted, it was being lived. When the followers of Jesus were first given the nickname 'Christians' in the city of Antioch ('It was at Antioch that the disciples were first. called Christians', Acts 11:26), the reference must have been primarily to their distinctive style of life rather than to the beliefs they professed.

We learn from the Gospels that Jesus himself had insisted on the practical effect of his teaching. These early Christians listened in their worship to extracts from what were to become our four Gospels, and must have heard often about the call to be the light that everyone can see, the salt that gives flavour to life and preserves it from corruption, the leaven that works quietly from within. They would also hear about the farmer's two sons, one of whom professed obedience to his father but did nothing while the other, making no such profession, got on with the job. The words would ring in their ears: 'Why do you call me, "Lord, Lord," and don't do what I tell you?' (Luke 6:46) Letters from the apostles like John, Peter, and James kept reminding them of the fact that they were called to demonstrate their acceptance of the Good News by a way of living. 'If someone says, "I love God," but hates his brother, he is a liar. For he cannot love God, whom he has not seen, if he does not love his brother, whom he has seen. This, then, is the command that Christ gave us: he who loves God must love his brother also' (1 John 4:20, 21). 'My brothers! What good is it for someone to say, "I have faith," if his actions do not prove it? Can that faith save him? Suppose there are brothers or sisters who need clothes and don't have enough to eat. What good is there in your saying to them, "God bless you! Keep warm and eat well!" – if you don't give them the necessities of life? So it is with faith: if it is alone and has no actions with it, then it is dead' (James 2:14-17). 'I appeal to you, my friends, as strangers and refugees in this world! Do not give in to bodily passions, which are always at war against the soul. Your conduct among the heathen should be so good that when they accuse you of being evildoers they will have to recognize your good deeds, and so praise God on the Day of his coming' (1 Peter 2:11, 12). It is remarkable that when the word 'Christianity' came into use it was known simply as 'the Way'. Those who believed the Good News were enlisted as followers of the Way – and that Way clearly was a style of life that distinguished the Christians from their pagan neighbours. So from the beginning ethical questions loomed large, and Paul's letters were found to contain not only general statements about the content of the new life in Christ but specific answers to moral questions raised by the new Christian conscience.

Once again we have to keep in mind the spontaneous, *ad hoc* nature of this correspondence. Just as it is really impossible to erect a complete system of dogmatics on the basis of the contents of these letters, so it is unwise to attempt to build from them a complete ethical system comparable to the works of Plato, Aristotle, Aquinas, or Kant. What we can find in the letters is (1) Paul's burning conviction that becoming a man or woman 'in Christ', being a member of this new community, must result in a new way of life, (2) constant references to the new moral dynamic let loose in the world and in the hearts of believers which he calls the Holy Spirit, the Spirit of Christ, the Spirit of life, and (3) specific words of advice on questions that were troubling the churches.

We have seen that Paul had no illusions about the

young churches to whom he was writing, and was well aware that many new Christians had neither made a clean break with their pagan past nor had shown much evidence of what he called the 'fruit of the Spirit'. Yet he always addressed them as in a peculiar sense 'God's holy people, who belong to him in union with Christ Jesus' (1 Corinthians 1:2), and could bestow the highest titles upon them even while castigating them for their lapses and their betrayals. This gives us an insight into the unique nature of Christian ethics as understood by Paul and the other apostles. The Way was never understood as a code of conduct against which the success or failure of Christians and churches could be measured. It was not an ethical system which people embraced because they thought it better than any of its rivals. It was a revolution of the spirit in which a man or woman renounced all claims to moral achievement, acknowledged that they were sinners, and set out to live a life of thankful response to the grace of God in the image of Jesus Christ. Paul was naturally distressed by conduct that belied this experience of grace, but he never ceased to treat the sincere baptized believer as one who had been called to the new life in Christ and was a member of his Body. Time and again he reminded them of their new birthright in the Christian faith. 'When anyone is joined to Christ he is a new being; the old is gone, the new has come' (2 Corinthians 5:17). 'It does not matter at all whether or not one is circumcised. What does matter is being a new creature' (Galatians 6:15). 'Get rid of your old self, which made you live as you used to – the old self that was being destroyed by its deceitful desires. Your hearts and minds must be made completely new. You must put on the new self, which is created in God's likeness, and reveals itself in the true life that is upright and holy' (Ephesians 4:22-4). He combines a clear-eyed recognition that there was some quite spectacular sinning going on in these churches with constant reminders of their new status in Christ. Thus he finds it possible to write to the Colossians, 'Do not lie to one another' and to add in the same breath, 'because you have put off the old self with its habits, and have put on the new self.'

The same kind of reasoning is to be found when he writes to the Corinthians who were up to all kinds of mischief ('sexual immorality among you so terrible that not even the heathen would be guilty of it,' he writes in a moment of fury). 'It is not right for you to be proud! You know the saying, "A little bit of yeast makes the whole batch of dough rise." You must take out this old yeast of sin so that you will be entirely pure. Then you will be like a new batch of dough without any yeast, as indeed I know you actually are.' He may be referring to the necessity of expelling a particularly blatant sinner from the fellowship, but note his extraordinary confidence in telling these people that they 'actually are' the pure community of God. It is this basic conviction that underlies all Paul's ethics. He believed in driving home the fact that a Christian is a forgiven sinner called to a life of purity and love, and all his ethical admonitions proceed from the assumption that above all we need to be reminded of what we are in Christ. It is the Christian version of *noblesse oblige*, and has always been the true dynamic of those who live by grace. The Christian moral imperative has accordingly been summarized in the paradoxical admonition: 'Become what you are!'

Unless there had indeed been a radically new element in the Christian ethic it is most unlikely that the Church would have moved so fast and so far in the first centuries of its existence. One has the impression that a somewhat tired world of which Gibbon succinctly remarked that 'the various modes of worship, which prevailed in the Roman world, were all considered by the people as equally true; by the philosopher, as equally false; and by the magistrate, as equally useful' was suddenly confronted by a network of religious communities in which common people, philosophers, and magistrates found a common conviction, experienced a completely new kind of love, and found a revolutionary moral dynamic. Since our modern world has shown some signs of reverting to the condition described by Gibbon, we could profit by a study of this Christian ethic as revealed in the letters of Paul and the other apostles.

Our understanding of the letters at this point has been confused by the traditions of 'Christendom' in which many of us were reared. By 'Christendom' I mean the culture that arose in the West as a result of centuries of Church dominance not only in religion but in science, the arts, law, and morals. Even though Christendom has virtually disappeared, and there are few nations left where the Church can impose its views, most of us live in a culture that has been profoundly influenced by Christian ideas and where at least lip-service is paid to Christian ethics. Therefore, until comparatively recently, the distinction between Christian and secular morality has been blurred and Church members in countries like Britain or the United States were not normally conscious of belonging to a community that professed totally different standards and motivations from those of its neighbours. In fact, it was common for those who had lost contact with the churches to insist that they still believed in the Christian ethic and even to claim that they practised it – a claim that the instructed church-goer is very loath to make. (There was a kind of reverse Pharisaism in operation whereby it was the one who stayed away from church who often claimed to be a 'better Christian' than those who went.)

In Europe, and to a lesser degree, in North America the situation has been rapidly changing. There is now an increasingly vociferous non-Christian, or even anti-Christian lobby that makes itself heard on every moral question, and it is quite common for discussions to take place, privately or publicly, in which acute ethical problems are considered without any reference to Christian convictions. I have listened to a panel of academics talking for several hours on the future of marriage without anyone even suggesting that the Christian Church had a point of view on the subject that might possibly be worth considering. The media in Europe and America still offer some space for the voice of the Church to be heard in services of worship but it is by and large a secularist philosophy that dominates the discussion of our way of life. Christians are being thrust back to a position where we can better understand the tensions Paul had in mind when writing to those first-century churches. In this sense the letters can speak more powerfully to us than to our forefathers who were able to take for granted a fairly general acceptance, at least in theory, of the Christian ethical tradition.

Can we now determine from the letters just what was really new about the ethics of the Christian Church? We have little more than scraps of material from which to learn about the actual shape and motivation of the Way to which Christians were now committed. There is nothing here comparable to a massive ethical system such as was offered at the time by the Stoics or Epicureans, or a detailed code of conduct for adherents to the new faith. The letters, together with the Gospels, offered the raw materials from which in time the great thinkers of the Church did create works of moral theology that were as intellectually imposing as any non-Christian systems before or since. They sprang out of the living situation of churches under great stress and the time for formulation and reflection was not yet. The reason for the absence of even a minimal code-book of ethical advice for Christian converts, however, brings us at once to the heart of the Good News and the way of life that issued from it.

For a code-book means law; and Paul is never tired of telling his new Christians that 'we know that a man is put right with God only through faith in Jesus Christ, never by doing what the Law requires.' He was acutely aware that the teachings of Jesus and his apostles could very soon be turned into a new kind of religious legalism as stringent and crushing as that from which Paul himself had been emancipated. If he had offered to these churches a manual of behaviour in which the Christian could find his duty spelled out in every imaginable situation, he would have betrayed the very freedom he had found in Christ. The only law he now acknowledged as totally binding on the Christian is what he calls 'the law of the Spirit, which brings us life in union with Christ Jesus'. This is the law which Jesus proclaimed – the law of love which is, in fact, the end of all legalism. For the law of the Spirit of life, he says, 'has set me free from the law of sin and death' (Romans 8:2). He was determined that those who had realized that they were saved by grace and not by keeping the Law should go on to live by grace and not by a slavish obedience to the letter of the Law. The new covenant, he insists (2 Corinthians 3:6) 'consists not of a written law, but of the Spirit. The written law brings death, but the Spirit gives life.' It is not only theologically that he proclaims the doctrine of grace, but ethically. This is why he scolds those who, having known the freedom that comes with the acceptance of the crucified and risen Saviour, lapsed into a new legalism almost at once. 'You foolish Galatians! Who put a spell on you? Right before your eyes you had a plain description of the death of Jesus on the cross! Tell me just this one thing: did you receive God's Spirit by doing what the Law requires, or by hearing and believing the Gospel? How can you be so foolish! You began by God's Spirit; do you now want to finish by your own power?' (Galatians 3:1-3)

It is not surprising that flaming words like these have served to arouse the Church in every century since they were written. For the temptation of the Christian to lapse into legalism is immensely powerful and over the years every segment of the Church – Catholic, Orthodox, Protestant – has developed its own kind. The rigid ritualist with his slavish adherence to ecclesiastical rules, the fighting fundamentalist with his narrow certainties and list of taboos, the doctrinaire liberal with his demand for action according to his party lines – all are examples of a lapse from grace. For Paul the centre of all Christian ethics is a living response to the grace that meets us in Christ, a thankful acceptance of the fact that we are forgiven sinners not morally superior persons, and the freedom of a life controlled by the Holy Spirit.

Living by grace rules out the arrogance that can result from a consciousness of having kept the moral law, immortally expressed by the man who 'stood apart from himself and prayed, "I thank you, God, that I am not greedy, dishonest, or immoral, like everybody else; I thank you that I am not like that tax collector. I fast two days every week, and I give you one tenth of all my income" ' (Luke 18:11, 12). That Paul himself had to struggle against this temptation is apparent from some of his more lofty remarks about his erring brethren, but we continually find him pulling himself up and adding touches like 'in this matter of boasting I am really talking

like a fool' (2 Corinthians 11:17) or, after his claim to
have been personally called by the living Christ to be an
apostle, 'I am the least of all the apostles – I do not even
deserve to be called an apostle, because I persecuted
God's church. But by God's grace I am what I am'
(1 Corinthians 15:9, 10). He inculcates this same spirit
of humility as he reminds all church members of their
status as forgiven sinners with no claim on God, and is
not slow to recall the vices from which Christ had
rescued them (Ephesians 2:1-3).

With this essential humility goes a spirit of constant
thankfulness. Since many have the impression that Paul
was a somewhat stern moralist and that he spilled a good
deal of ink in castigating his converts for their lapses,
it might be surprising to be told that at the heart of
Paul's ethics is gratitude and thanksgiving. But that is
the note that rings through the letters. Nearly every one
of them opens with a celebration of the grace of God
and an outpouring of gratitude not only for his goodness
but for the faith, hope, and love that he sees developing
in his Christian congregations. Then you will notice
that the specific pieces of moral advice are nearly always
to be found at the end of the letters. It is only after he
has reminded them of all that God has done, and of their
glorious freedom as his sons and daughters, that he
indicates how their gratitude should spill over into particular acts of Christian compassion, restraint, and
generosity. Most of his letters are, as it were, in the
indicative mood: God has done thus and thus for you
in Christ. Only after he has aroused the spirit of thankfulness does he begin to use the imperative: Do this; don't
do that.

Since Paul himself uses occasional illustrations to
convey his meaning (although he has nothing comparable
to the sparkling parables of Jesus and is apt at times to
labour over an allegory from the Old Testament [Gala-
tians 4:21-31] or run into trouble with a metaphor
[Romans 11:16-18]), it might be helpful to use a contemporary picture to shed light on the root of his ethics. The
difference between what he calls living by law and living by
grace is like the difference between the experience of a child
reared in an institution and one reared in a good home.

Let's say the institution is well-run, just, and strict; and the home is loving, firm, and forgiving. The one child will tend to grow up either rebellious or submissive. He will perceive life in terms of rewards and punishments. The other has a good chance of developing into a happy, responsive, imaginative person with a spontaneous appreciation of what is good and true. Assuming that the moral standards of the institution and the home are roughly similar, the point is that the response of the two children is entirely different. If the first child grows up submissive these moral precepts will be a kind of chain around his conscience: he will obey largely from fear of the consequences. He is, as Paul would say, under the Law. If the second child turns out well he will obey the precepts almost without knowing he is doing so: he will be responding spontaneously to the example of those he loves. He is, as Paul would say, under grace. Another illustration could be the response we make to two different kinds of teacher. There is the one who says: 'There's the task to be done: now go and do it.' There's the other who takes time to sit alongside to encourage and explain. We may work for them both, but there is no question as to which influences us and inspires us in what we are learning. What we have learned by grace has a way of staying with us, and giving us pleasure, while what we have learned by law is often resented and easily forgotten.

Paul's ethics as a Christian were inspired by the inner presence of the Spirit of Christ far more than by what he had learned of the ethical teachings of the historic Jesus. If he does not cite these often in his letters it is not because he was unfamiliar with, say, the Sermon on the Mount, but because he wanted to introduce his converts to the personal presence of the Lord rather than to load upon them a new Law to be followed. He seized on the contrast which Jesus himself drew between a slavish obedience to a series of commandments and the freedom of the true children of God. He knew himself to be the forgiven Prodigal rather than the grudging Elder Brother, and it was the ethic of the restored Prodigal he commended to his churches. The Way was thus no new Law but an experience of joyful acceptance of grace and a free, spontaneous, and infectious response to the Spirit of Christ.

We have seen that his rejection of legalism did not mean that theologically he had no use for the concept of Law. In the same way his rejection of ethical legalism did not mean that the Law had no place whatever in the Christian Way. It is wrong to suppose that Paul's enthusiasm for the new life in Christ led him to repudiate either the moral commandments of the Old Testament or the best that he found in contemporary pagan ethics. He shows himself, of course, profoundly steeped in the ethics of Judaism, but is also aware of, and respectful towards, some of the ideals of the Greek and Roman traditions which guided the best minds and spirits of his age. In other words, he was not throwing overboard the highest moral precepts of mankind to embrace and proclaim an entirely new way of living. When, for instance, he has just written to the Philippians about the secret of Christian living – 'Don't worry about anything, but in all your prayers ask God for what you need, always asking him with a thankful heart. And God's peace, which is far beyond human understanding, will keep your hearts and minds safe, in union with Jesus' (Philippians 4:6) – he goes on immediately to remind them of moral virtues that have been commended by the great teachers of every time and place – 'In conclusion, my brothers, fill your minds with those things that are good and deserve praise: things that are true, noble, right, pure, lovely, and honourable' (v. 8).

Unlike some modern exponents of Christian ethics he saw the Law as the expression of the will of God, as the norm to be respected and revered, as the judge of our sinfulness, and as a guide to our perplexities. He had indeed found no salvation through the Law, but it had been, he said, 'in charge of us until Christ came' (Galatians 3:24), and he realized that the Law was totally fulfilled by Christ who incarnated the perfect love of God and one's neighbour. James Moffatt once wrote of the Judaizing party whom Paul was fighting: 'They had made the Law their Christ, and God intended Christ to be the Law.' There is no sign that Paul ever used the argument that, say, one of the Ten Commandments could be abrogated in the name of something called Christian love. He *might* have declared that a Christian, faced with the choice of two inescapable evils, would break one Law to preserve another; but he would surely then have him say: 'God help me; as a sinner I can do no other', rather than exult in some illusory freedom to defy the norm. He is never afraid to use the expressions 'right' and 'wrong', 'moral' and 'immoral', and nowhere in his letters does he hint at the existence of such a thing as 'the new morality'.

There are signs in his letters of the existence of these grey areas of moral decision where Christians in every generation have found themselves in disagreement. We have already had a look at some of these battles of conscience. We can take comfort from the thought that the apostle recognized that there could be no unanimity on all points (and perhaps too from the thought that he himself on occasion came down on the wrong side). We can listen again to the passages in which he commends a frank airing of differences 'in the Spirit', and shows that part of the process of 'becoming mature', 'reaching to the very height of Christ's full stature' is 'speaking the truth in a spirit of love'. That, he says, is how 'we must grow up in every way to Christ, who is the head' (Ephesians 4:13, 15).

Of enormous importance to Paul's ethics was the existence and nature of the Church. In spite of his dominant personality, in spite of the profoundly personal nature of his own relationship to Christ, and in spite of his strenuous advocacy of a union with Christ on the part of every individual, his was no merely personal ethic. He saw the Way as a road we travel with others. Most of his letters were to churches and even those to individuals carried always the imprint of the Christian community. Timothy is given detailed instructions as to how a church leader should behave (1 Timothy 3); Titus is told in no uncertain terms about his responsibilities as a church officer; Philemon receives greetings to 'the church that meets in your house'; and it seems that Paul never wrote a line to any Christian without the thought of the community of which they were a part. It is strange that Paul has often been seen as the prophet of Christian individualism as if he was dedicated to conveying the Good News as a personal message to each man or woman and saw their Christian growth as something that happened in isolation from the community of believers. His letters have often been read in this way and the impression has been given that Paul was like a guru who attracts individual followers but has no interest in communal worship or communal action.

An attentive reading of the letters shatters any such idea. Paul was no Christian guru dispensing the enlightenment that he had found. He was from first to last, by his own admission, a slave of Christ and servant of his Church; and he wrote to Christians never forgetting that they were incorporated in the community he called the Body of Christ. He had not the slightest interest in creating a new movement composed of individuals who felt attracted to him and his interpretation of the Good News. When he found that the Corinthians were forming parties – 'One says, "I am with Paul"; another, "I am with Apollos"; another, "I am with Peter"; and another, "I am with Christ" ' (1 Corinthians 1:12) – he exploded: 'Christ has been divided into groups! Was it Paul who died on the cross for you? Were you baptized as Paul's disciples?' For him the Church that Christ had brought into being towered beyond all sects and squabbles among Christians. It had been there before he ever became a Christian, and his conversion implied his baptism into the community of believers. There is no sign in his letters of the modern conception of the Church as a kind of afterthought, a getting-together of those who happened to share the same religious experience. It was not a mere convenience, a Christian club founded by the apostles and subject in every area to the whims of local leaders. From the very moment of his conversion he was aware that the Christ and his Church were so intimately linked that to be 'in Christ' was *ipso facto* to be a member of the Church. This accounts for the strange words Luke reports that he heard when he was struck down on the Damascus road in the middle of his campaign against the infant Church: 'Saul, Saul! Why do you persecute *me*?'

Since we are entangled today in a semantic web when-

ever we use the word 'church' – do we mean the building
on the corner, the people connected with it, the de-
nomination to which it belongs, the totality of Christians
in the world, or some mystical body in heaven and on
earth? – it is refreshing to find that Paul seems to know
only two different uses of the word. He speaks of *the
Church* meaning 'the people of God', the holy community
redeemed by Christ, founded on him, universal in its
scope, embracing the living and the dead, and destined
to be presented to God 'in all its beauty, pure and
faultless, without spot or wrinkle, or any other imperfection' (Ephesians 5:27). And he speaks of *the churches*
meaning the local community of Christians in places
like those to whom he addressed his letters. He knows
nothing whatever of intermediate groupings called de-
nominations and could not have conceived of our ad-
jectival 'churches' named after their system of government, like Episcopalian, Presbyterian, and Congregational, or after personalities like Luther and Wesley.
Still less could he have dreamed of the possibility of
anyone inventing a new church – even if it were to be
called the One True Orthodox Bible-believing Holy
Church of God. A church for Paul was not something
to be created by Christians: it was there already and
simply awaited its local manifestation. One doesn't invent
a church: one finds it – or rather, it finds us.

When speaking of *the* Church Paul ransacks his
vocabulary and supply of metaphors to describe its
wonder and its glory. Even when he does not use the
word, the sound of the great company of believers, those
who have been 'rescued . . . from the power of darkness
and brought . . . safe into the kingdom of his dear Son'
(Colossians 1:13), 'God's people', 'the Israel of God'
(Galatians 6:16, KJV), the 'fellow-citizens with God's
people, and members of the family of God' (Ephesians
2:19), rings through every page that he wrote. His
favourite metaphors help us to understand the power of
his churchmanship, the sustaining belief that he had in
the reality and endurance, the unity and variety, of this
new fellowship in Christ. He draws his analogies from
the fields of architecture and anatomy. A third analogy,
beloved of other New Testament writers, from the mar-

riage relationship – the Church being the 'Bride of Christ' – he avoids for reasons about which we might hazard a guess.

The architectural metaphor is that of the building of which the foundation is Christ ('For God has already placed Jesus Christ as the one and only foundation, and no other foundation can be laid' [1 Corinthians 3:11]) or the apostolic witness to Christ with Christ himself as the cornerstone ('You, too, are built upon the foundation by the apostles and prophets, the cornerstone being Christ Jesus himself' [Ephesians 2:20]). In this metaphor the stress is upon solidity and permanence of the foundation (or cornerstone) and also upon the upbuilding of the structure according to the divine plan. Hence the word 'edification' (KJV) which, whatever it has come to mean in modern days, meant originally just that – upbuilding. Paul saw his own task as the kind of edification of the Church. He has authority 'to build you up . . . not to tear you down' (2 Corinthians 10:8) – a remark which Church leaders might take to heart in any age. His image of the ethical and spiritual progress of the members of the Church is of their being built up into the structure of this great temple of God. It is beautifully expressed in the letter to the Ephesians with the words: 'He is the one who holds the whole building together and makes it grow into a sacred temple in the Lord. In union with him you too are being built together with all the others into a house where God lives through his Spirit' (Ephesians 2:21, 22).

The anatomical metaphor is even richer. The Church is the body of which Christ is the head. 'The church is Christ's body, the completion of him who himself completes all things everywhere,' he writes to the Ephesians (1:23). 'He is the head of his body, the church,' he writes to the Colossians, and expands: 'he is the source of the body's life.' This is the most powerful metaphor ever devised to convey to us the relationship of Christ to his Church. It reminds us of the essential unity of the whole Christian community in heaven and on earth. It is the justification for using the word 'holy' when speaking of the Church. It is a warning both to those who tend to think of the Church in terms of some kind of human

contract, and to those who would like the Church to act
as if its leaders and councils had the wisdom and
authority of Christ himself. The body is holy for it is the
temple of the Spirit of Christ; but members of the body,
no matter how exalted, are to be totally subject to its
head. Paul elaborates this metaphor with great effect
when dealing with the rivalries of Christians in the
exercise of their spiritual gifts:

> For the body itself is not made up of only one part
> but of many parts. If the foot were to say, 'Because I
> am not a hand, I don't belong to the body,' that would
> not make it stop being a part of the body. And if the
> ear were to say, 'Because I am not an eye, I don't belong
> to the body,' that would not make it stop being a part
> of the body. If the whole body were just an eye, how
> could it hear? And if it were only an ear, how could it
> smell? As it is, however, God put every different part
> in the body just as he wished. There would not be a
> body if it were all only one part! As it is, there are
> many parts, and one body.
> So then, the eye cannot say to the hand, 'I don't
> need you!' Nor can the head say to the feet, 'Well, I
> don't need you!' On the contrary, we cannot do without
> the parts of the body that seem to be weaker; and those
> parts that we think aren't worth very much are the ones
> which we treat with greater care; while the parts of the
> body which don't look very nice receive special atten-
> tion, which the more beautiful parts of our body do not
> need. God himself has put the body together in such a
> way as to give greater honour to those parts that lack
> it. And so there is no division in the body, but all its
> different parts have the same concern for one another.
> If one part of the body suffers, all the other parts suffer
> with it; if one part is praised, all the other parts share
> its happiness.
> All of you, then, are Christ's body, and each one
> is a part of it.

(1 Corinthians 12:14–27)

This brings us from the Church to the churches. As
we have seen Paul never allows his lofty conception of

the holy people of God to blind him to the way these holy people sometimes behave within the all too human fellowship of the churches. It is this contrast that led a certain cynic to make this addition to the Nicene Creed: 'I believe in One, Holy, Catholic, and Apostolic Church – and regret that it doesn't exist.' Paul not only believed in its existence but in its power to help those 'sinners saved by grace' to be drawn towards the fulfilment of the great design of God. He knew that the Church, like its Lord, was incarnate. It consisted of very human human beings. The one holy catholic church existed in visible form. It was one for in spite of squabbles and divisions no one had yet suggested that it could be divided. It was holy, for the Spirit of Christ was active in the new community. It was catholic, for no distinctions or privileges of race, rank, or culture were recognized in it. It was apostolic, for the authority of the apostolic teaching and preaching was everywhere acknowledged. It is impossible to gather from Paul's correspondence just how these qualities of the universal Church were expressed in the government of the Church. There were, besides the apostles, other officers called 'presbyters', 'bishops', 'deacons', 'evangelists' and 'teachers', but we have no way of knowing exactly how these offices functioned, or their relative authority. We do know that there were councils which had authority over the whole Church, but how often they met and how much they controlled what happened locally we can only guess.

What we do know was that the Body of Christ existed in the form of local churches, and it was to them that these letters were written. Paul's opening formula is standard: 'to the church of God which is at Corinth, at Thessalonica, at Colossae, at Rome . . .' Each of these was a local incarnation of the one Church catholic, and it is worth noting that Paul uses this phrase and not 'to the Corinth church, to the Roman church'. If we had preserved this way of thinking we might have been spared some of the splintering and sectarianism that has occurred whenever a local church begins to imagine that it is *the* Church.

Paul had an immense affection for these groups of Christians, some of whom must have been comparatively small, although they gave him endless worries. (After listing his trials and sufferings as a missionary of Christ – beatings, stonings, shipwrecks, hunger, thirst, and lack of sleep – he can't help adding, 'And, not to mention other things, every day I am under the pressure of my concern for all the churches. When someone is weak, then I feel weak too; when someone is led into sin, I am filled with distress.') It is this constant care for the members of these churches, and his insistence that it is part of Church membership to care deeply for the others, ('Help carry one another's burdens, and in this way you will obey the law of Christ' [Galatians 6:2]) that brings home to us how warm and real a thing was this *Koinonia* (communion, fellowship) of which the whole New Testament speaks. It was much more than an occasional greeting at times of worship, or a passing contribution to help the hungry and the poor. It was a sustaining and uplifting force that enabled individual Christians to stay by their beliefs, to grow in Christian hope and love, and to come through the trials and disappointments of their personal lives. At this point these letters might bring a challenging and healing word to the churches of our time, and to those outside who are groping for just such a sustaining and invigorating community.

6. HIS TEACHING ABOUT HUMAN DESTINY AND LIFE ETERNAL

A fascinating question that arises out of our reading of the correspondence of Paul is: To what extent did he interpret the Good News as an assurance of life beyond the grave for the individual and a future triumph for that way of life which the New Testament calls the Kingdom of God? At the time these letters were written there was as much confusion, scepticism, dogmatism, passion, and indifference about 'eternal life' as there is today. In Judaism the endless argument between Pharisee and Sadducee went on, the one asserting the truth of resurrection and the other denying it. The philosophers tended to reject all popular notions of life after death. The average citizen was no longer sustained by the local religion of his ancestors, and the pagan cults had never really offered much solid hope for individual survival in another world. The mystery religions spoke of a union with the divine that held promise of immortality but, in the tradition of eastern mysticism, they conceived of it in terms of absorption into the divine being rather than as an extension and fulfilment of the life of the individual. Although there were some who professed indifference as to whether or not this is the only life we have, there was just as much curiosity, not to say yearning, associated with this topic as there is today.

The evidence is that the Good News about Jesus Christ made a tremendous impact with its insistence that it is possible here and now to be assured of eternal life. Every New Testament writer speaks with total conviction about the power of God to raise us up beyond death to share in the immortality of Christ. In their preaching the apostles and their successors had no hesitation in declaring that the new life that came by faith and was expressed in the ceremony of baptism carried in it the pledge of continued existence in a heavenly world. While the Christian preaching seems to have been restrained in its descriptions of such a life beyond, and did not deal in promises as to any particular kind of 'pie in the sky', it was firm in asserting the basic assurance expressed in the prayer of Jesus: 'I want them to be with me where I am.' (John 17:24) Although many of these new Christians had already some kind of belief in an eternal world before their conversion, there is no question about the source of their new and radiant conviction: it came from their belief in the resurrection of Jesus and communion with their risen Lord. With this preaching there was another powerful testimony to their belief in a world to come. The word 'martyr' simply means witness, and its new meaning came from the fact that these men and women witnessed to their assurance about life eternal by their readiness to yield their lives in the cause of Christ. Paul himself was present at the scene described by Luke (Acts 7:59, 60) when the first martyr, Stephen, was stoned to death, and must have heard his dying words: 'Lord Jesus, receive my spirit!' It was because of the impressive sight of thousands being willing to die for their faith in total conviction that another life awaited them that it could later be written that 'the blood of the martyrs became the seed of the Church.'

We shall expect, then, to find in the letters of Paul constant echoes of this soaring hope, and perhaps some expounding of its rationale. And so we do – but much more often in incidental remarks and assumptions, in the general tone and tenor of the letters, and in revealing asides than in disquisitions about human destiny and eternal life. We have seen already how impossible it is to construct a coherent and elaborate system of dogma, or of ethics, from these letters. In the same way we must not look for a formal and consistent system of eschatology. (Now that this word has slipped out, let me briefly note that it is a convenient code-word used by theologians for the doctrines of what are called the 'Last Things' or 'End Things', *eschaton* being a Greek word meaning 'last in time', or 'the end of time'. Under the heading of Eschatology come subjects like death, resurrection, eternal life, heaven, hell, judgement – all that we are dealing with in this chapter. The word is now filtering into the speech of the sophisticated: thinking or living 'eschatologically' being a fashionable way of expressing the sense of an imminent end. When Dr Johnson remarked: 'Depend upon it, Sir, when a man knows he is to be hanged in a fortnight, it concentrates his mind wonderfully,' he was referring to eschatological thinking, and there are many today who feel that the hidden threat of the bomb is inducing a certain kind of eschatological living. After the interlude of a couple of centuries you might say that eschatology is 'back in'.) There is much material in Paul's letters to help us to think and live eschatologically in the Christian sense but nothing resembling a manual of authoritative beliefs concerning the exact course of future events or what Reinhold Niebuhr used to call 'the furniture of heaven or the temperature of hell'.

It may even come as a surprise to some that Paul has so little to say about the rewards of heaven and the punishments of hell. It is still a popular myth that the Bible is full of such promises and warnings. In fact, the entire Old Testament has practically nothing to say about life in a world beyond and the apostles deal very little in threats and promises about the future state. It is in the recorded words of Jesus that we find by far the most references to heaven and hell, but even he warned against any idle curiosity (Matthew 22:23-33; 24:36) and used the thought of eternity to emphasize the decisive importance of this present life. Paul expounds his Good News as one who is absolutely certain that the life of humanity and of the individual is not bounded by the final chill of death but moves toward a fulfilment in another dimension under the sovereignty of God. Yet, he is as far as could be from the attitude of the slick pedlar of luscious heavenly rewards.

Interest in the question of what lies ahead is normally divided between a natural curiosity about what may happen to us after death (I am sceptical about the frequent remark: 'I don't care what happens to me.' How many would also be willing to say about the death of someone dear: 'I don't care what has happened to him or her'?) and a wondering about the destiny of the

human race, not to mention the ultimate goal and purpose, if any, of the entire universe. To begin with the
latter question: What did Paul find in the Good News
that gave him some convictions about the future course
of events for the human race, and even the ultimate
meaning and destiny of all creation?

The first answer must be that he was not a confirmed
crystal-gazer and shows no signs of that mania for precise
prediction of coming events that has bedevilled sections
of the Church in every age. Those in our day who delight
in scouring the Bible for signs and codes predicting what
will happen in the year 2000 or what Mr Kissinger is up
to right now in the Middle East, seldom find much
material in the letters of Paul. They are much happier
delving into the apocalyptic symbols of the Books of
Daniel or Revelation (which is why that shrewd French-
man John Calvin would have liked to exclude these books
from our Bibles). Nowhere in the letters does Paul go
out on a limb with predictions about what is going to
happen to the Roman Empire, or cryptically indicate
that he knows something about 1914 or 1945. He doesn't
even know where he himself is going to be from one
month to the next or what eventually will happen to him.
He tells the Roman Christians that he intends to go to
Spain after he visits them (Romans 15:28) but no one
knows whether he ever made the journey. Occasionally
he has a hunch that there is danger ahead, or that he
ought to change his plans, but he never talks as one to
whom destiny has been divinely revealed. He refers, in
a passage to which we will return, to his complete un-
certainty while in prison as to whether he will be executed
or set free. Everywhere he speaks as a man who is content
to live by the grace of God and leave the future to him.

Yet, Paul was very far from being a fatalist or cynic.
In every line he wrote there breathes the conviction of a
believing Jew that all things are in the hands of the
sovereign God. So passionately does he believe nothing
in human destiny is sheer accident that he is not afraid
to use the bogey-word 'predestinate'. (The Greek word,
so translated in the King James version, is paraphrased
in Today's English Version. 'Having predestinated us
unto the adoption of children by Jesus Christ to himself'

becomes 'God had already decided that through Jesus Christ he would bring us to himself as his sons' – which makes Paul's meaning plainer for us today [Ephesians 1:5].) Predestination was for him not a fatalistic assumption that 'what will be will be' (there is no sign of that in either his letters or his life) but a burning conviction that our salvation depends on God alone.

With this controlling belief, Paul had also inherited from his Judaism certain modes of thinking and expression concerning things to come. To understand the language he uses when writing about 'Last Things' we need to know a little about the apocalyptic literature that abounded in his day. This reflected a religious mood that turned from the preoccupation with living by God's commandments in this present world to speculation about God's intervention from on high. It was induced by a pessimism about the possibility of a restored and triumphant Israel under some new King David, and a mystic belief in the imminence of the advent of the Messiah. The heavenly Deliverer was not conceived of as a warrior like Moses or Joshua, or a dazzling potentate like Solomon, but as a supernatural figure, often referred to as 'the Son of Man' (Daniel 7:13, 14) who would appear in the clouds and usher in the Kingdom of God. This kind of thinking flourished in communities like those associated with the Dead Sea Scrolls and nourished in the hearts of many Jews the burning hope that God was about to intervene in human history and vindicate his people. For many religious leaders the apocalyptic writings were suspect and regarded as subversive of the orderly teaching and practice of the Law, but their influence was widespread. The scenario of the apocalyptic speakers and writers generally included a period of intense conflict in which the powers of evil reached their climax with the appearance of an anti-Christ, the Man of Sin, some kind of final conflict (called Armageddon, from the hill of Megiddo where it was to take place), and a glorious triumph of the Messiah with the legions of the Just. These figures, and the accompanying symbolism of clouds, fire, earthquakes, and storms, were familiar to many Christian converts and have found their way into New Testament writings such as the apocalyptic chapters in the Gospels (e.g., Mark 13), the letters of Paul, particularly to the Thessalonians, and, above all, the Book of Revelation.

To recognize this is not to dismiss all such passages as relics of an archaic religiosity, a strange aberration that can say nothing to us. When we allow for the fact that occasional words and symbols will be obscure to us and certainly should not be exploited by literal western minds today in the interests of some theory about the precise nature of Christ's return and the end of the world, we should be open to the truth behind the images – that human history does not steadily evolve towards the Kingdom of God but is subject to radical, not to say irrational, disturbances from another dimension; and that the human race, like each one of us, will come to a terminus – which will be neither a bang nor a whimper but the judgement of God.

The apocalyptic element in Paul's letters centres on the future coming of Christ. In his earliest extant letters (to the Thessalonians) he makes full use of the language and imagery of apocalypse and is clearly writing to those who believed, as he did, that the Lord Jesus would very soon return in glory. We have already considered how this expectation coloured some of his ethical advice (hence the expression 'interim ethics' meaning a way of life recommended for those in the brief interim between the first and second coming of Jesus), and how it motivated him in his fantastic scurry across the whole Roman world with the Good News. It has been much debated whether or not Paul changed his views, and his expectations, in later years when it began to appear that the return of Christ might be long delayed. We can form our own impression as we read the later books. There is nothing in the letters to the Philippians or Colossians that resembles his vivid picture of the *parousia* (the Greek word used to indicate the appearing of Christ in glory) in the Thessalonian letters, but we still find him saying, for instance, that 'we eagerly wait for our Saviour to come from heaven, the Lord Jesus Christ' (Philippians 3:20) and 'your real life is Christ, and when he appears, then you too will appear with him and share his glory!' It may be that he had come to believe that the 'appearing' of Christ was something that would happen at our individual death as well as at the ultimate death of the human race.

The importance of this theme, for him and for us, lies in the conviction that, to use the language of the Revelation, Christ is the Alpha and Omega, the beginning and the end. Just as he wrote to the Colossians that 'by him God created everything in heaven and on earth' (Colossians 1:16) so he wrote to the Philippians that 'in honour of the name of Jesus, all beings in heaven, on earth, and in the world below will fall on their knees, and all will openly proclaim that Jesus Christ is the Lord, to the glory of God the Father' (Philippians 2:10, 11). The Ephesian letter has this stupendous affirmation about the cosmic significance of Christ: 'God's plan, which he will complete when the time is right, is to bring all creation together, everything in heaven and on earth, with Christ as head.' On this theme of Christ as the Omega-point (to use the language of Teilhard de Chardin whose evolutionary philosophy envisages this as the culminating point of 'the phenomenon of man') J. S. Stewart has these eloquent words (*A Man in Christ*, pp. 317-18): 'Well might the Church of apostolic days, knowing the strength of the enemy and seeing its own advent hope receding down the multiplying years, begin to wonder whether the kingdom dream would ever be fulfilled, or whether the new creation of Christ would perish in the desert far from the goal, and chaos and ancient night return. To this question – which is as haunting in the twentieth century as in the first – Paul's answer is clear and definite. The world is not moving on to chaos: it is moving on to Christ.'

If we should begin to wonder, at this point, if Paul has not indeed become a Jesus-worshipper in the sense of having replaced the God of his fathers by another deity, we might ponder the way in which he never fails to relate the Son to the Father, and to preserve the monotheism in which he was raised. The passage in which he summarizes his convictions about the ultimate destiny of the human race must remain for most, if not all, Christians the anchor of our hope and the fixed point for our convictions about the End. 'Then the end will come,' he wrote in 1 Corinthians (15:24-8). 'Christ will overcome all spiritual rulers, authorities, and powers, and hand over the Kingdom to God the Father. For Christ must rule until God defeats all enemies and puts them under his feet . . . But when all things have been placed under Christ's rule, then he himself, the Son, will place himself under God, who placed all under him; and God will rule completely over all.'

To the many questions we might like to ask, such as: 'Will all the evil powers be totally destroyed or will they be relegated to a hell of separation from God or will they be ultimately converted unto him?' we can find no certain answers in these letters (or anywhere else, taking the Bible witness as a whole). The same agnosticism is to be commended when we turn to the question of the fate of individuals which is our next topic. Christian scholars are still divided as to the destiny of the wicked, or the fate of the unbeliever. Probably, as no answer can be given to the question of the origin of evil, so no answer can be given to the question of its fate. Paul does speak of a judgement: 'For all of us must appear before Christ, to be judged by him. Each one will receive what he deserves, according to what he has done, good or bad, in his bodily life' (2 Corinthians 5:10). Nowhere does he speak of 'hell' but he can speak of an erring brother who will 'swell up with pride and be condemned, as the Devil was', (1 Timothy 3:6) and he clearly holds 'condemnation' to be the alternative to salvation (Romans 8:1). Yet, there are statements that seem to imply a universal triumph of the Gospel through which all are saved, notably the words to the Corinthians: 'For just as all men die because of their union to Adam, in the same way all will be raised to life because of their union to Christ.' (1 Corinthians 15:22) Paul seemed to hold in tension, as perhaps all Christians must, both the belief that our response to Christ is free and all-important *and* the belief that through the sacrifice of the Cross and the raising of Christ from the dead the whole world has been redeemed.

In modern times, with our accent on the individual, the whole question of eternal life has tended to be seen much more in terms of what will happen to each one of us than of what the fate of the universe, or destiny of mankind, will be. In the earlier parts of the Old Testament, in other great religions of the world, and in many places today, there has been no such concern about the individual. For some faiths eternal life is, in fact, the elimination of one's own personality by absorption in the divine All, and in certain Christian traditions the thought of the eternal 'communion of saints' means much more than that of individual survival. But for most of us who are the heirs of a tradition which has stressed the unique value of each human being, the question of what happens to us personally after death is bound to concern us deeply. It is significant that it is where there is this stress upon the individual that spiritist phenomena and psychic research have had their greatest appeal, and equally significant that they have flourished in almost direct proportion to the muting of the Church's message about life beyond the grave.

For Paul the Good News contained an assurance of personal experience of eternal life that is just as strong as his convictions about the ultimate victory of Christ over the forces of sin and death. Indeed he sees that victory as the guarantee that those who are united to Christ will share in the eternity of God's love. The famous conclusion to the eighth chapter of the Roman letter reveals how he roots his personal conviction of life eternal in the triumph of Christ over all the powers – natural and supernatural, philosophical and psychological – that could rob us of this hope. 'For I am certain that nothing can separate us from his love: neither death nor life; neither angels nor other heavenly ruler or powers; neither the present nor the future; neither the world above nor the world below – there is nothing in all creation that will ever be able to separate us from the love of God which is ours through Christ Jesus our Lord.' That Paul was thinking, not only in cosmic terms about the triumph of Christ and the defeat of the evil powers but also of the fulfilment of the individual in this eternity of God's love can be deduced from his own deep concern for the very real people whom he knew and loved. One of the most remarkable features of these letters is the way in which he will switch from the great affirmations of the faith and soaring visions of the cosmic Christ to sending his greetings to Phoebe, Rufus, Persis, Hermas, and Julia. (The Roman letter, his most profoundly theological, names at least twenty-six people whom he remembers fondly in this way. If anyone asks why we should be bothered with these lists of long-dead Christians about whom we know nothing at all, the answer is that these names are themselves happy reminders that the Good News is not a theory for philosophers to discuss but a personal message addressed to people like you and me. It is when Paul writes 'Aquila and Priscilla and the church that meets in their house send warm Christian greetings' (1 Corinthians 16:19) or 'Greetings to Apelles, whose loyalty to Christ has been proved' (Romans 16:10) or 'Euodia and Syntyche, please, I beg you, try to agree as sisters in the Lord' (Philippians 4:2) or 'Luke, our dear doctor, and Demas send you their greetings' (Colossians 4:14) or 'Do your best to come to me soon. Demas fell in love with this present world and has deserted me; he has gone off to Thessalonica. Crescens went to Galatia, and Titus to Dalmatia. Only Luke is with me. Get Mark and bring him with you, because he can help me in the work. I sent Tychicus to Ephesus. When you come, bring my coat that I left in Troas with Carpus; bring the books too, and especially the ones made of parchment' – that we find ourselves introduced to a circle of real people (about whom our imaginations can dream without end) and can see Paul as a live, warm, caring human being who surely had these friends in mind when he wrote of human destiny and eternal life.

Like his Master, Paul seldom argued the case for eternal life. Just as Jesus based his assumption that there is a life beyond to be reckoned with on his assurance that to be in communion with God here is to be already in touch with the eternal (Luke 20:37, 38) so Paul sees the tie that binds him to God in Christ as one which death cannot break. And just as Jesus refused to offer any description of life in heaven, Paul never indulges in any speculation about conditions in a realm that is impossible for mortals to conceive. For him it is always sufficient that he will be 'with Christ' and for the rest he would be content to cite the scripture: 'What no man ever saw or heard, what no man ever thought could happen, is the very thing God prepared for those who love him.' (1 Corinthians 2:9) You will find in these letters no mention of pearly gates or golden pavements, and no suggestion that eternity will be spent in the drowsy boredom of eternal harping – a kind of everlasting unemployment. He does indeed allow himself to use the metaphor of the prize, since he is apt to compare the Christian life to an athletic contest. 'I have done my best in the race, I have run the full distance, I have kept the faith. And now the prize of victory is waiting for me, the crown of righteousness which the Lord, the righteous Judge, will give me on that Day – and not only to me, but to all those who wait with love for him to appear.' But this thought of heavenly reward, we must remember, can be paralleled by many statements of Jesus himself, and does not carry with it the notion that there will thereafter be nothing to do. And that Paul was far from a smug assumption that he had grasped all the Good News had to offer and was only waiting for his prize is revealed when he writes: 'Of course, brothers, I really do not think that I have already won it; the one thing I do, however, is to forget what is behind me and do my best to reach what is ahead. So I run straight towards the goal in order to win the prize, which is God's call through Christ Jesus to the life above' (Philippians 3:13, 14).

Again, like Jesus, he had a strong sense of what we might call 'the pull of the eternal'. He believed that the qualities the Christian seeks here and now exist in their perfection in heaven and that we are moved towards that goal by a contemplation of the eternal and a proleptic sharing in its glory. 'You have been raised to life with Christ,' he writes to the Colossians (3:1). 'Set your hearts, then, on the things that are in heaven, where Christ sits on his throne at the right side of God.' He would be thoroughly in sympathy with the writer of the letter to the Hebrews who saw the Christian athlete as both keeping his eyes on Jesus and being encouraged by the host of heavenly spectators. 'As for us, we have this large crowd of witnesses round us. Let us rid ourselves, then, of everything that gets in the way, and the sin which holds on to us so tightly, and let us run with determination the race that lies before us. Let us keep our eyes fixed on Jesus, on whom our faith depends from beginning to end' (Hebrews 12:1, 2). The New Testament heaven is a lively place whence flows a stream of spiritual energy for all who are facing in that direction.

It is this conviction that enables Paul to declare that no amount of suffering and trial in this life can outweigh the astounding experiences that await the believer in the world beyond. In a most powerful passage he speaks of the agonies that most of us have at some time to endure, and of the sober fact of the decaying of our physical powers, and then shows why none of these things should ultimately dismay or crush the Christian believer. 'We are often troubled, but not crushed; sometimes in doubt, but never in despair; there are many enemies, but we are never without a friend; and though badly hurt at times, we are not destroyed' (2 Corinthians 4:8, 9). 'Even though our physical being is gradually decaying, yet our spiritual being is renewed day after day. And this small and temporary trouble we suffer will bring us a tremendous and eternal glory, much greater than the trouble. For we fix our attention, not on things that are seen, but on things that are unseen. What can be seen lasts only for a time; but what cannot be seen lasts forever.'

There is no doubt whatever about the chief source of Paul's blazing conviction about the reality of the life eternal. It was not a Platonic belief in these things that are seen which are but a shadow of the eternal things that are not seen. It was not the late Hebrew conception that we sometimes sing in church: 'He hath eternal life implanted in the soul.' It was not his training as a Pharisee in the doctrine of Resurrection. It was supremely and overwhelmingly his belief in the Resurrection of Jesus Christ. This is reflected in almost every reference he makes to life beyond the grave, and is elaborated with unusual passion and persuasiveness in the famous fifteenth chapter of the first letter to the Corinthians.

Addressing those in the church who apparently were denying the hope of a resurrection (even on this point there were sceptics in the Church from the beginning!) he writes: 'Now, since our message is that Christ has been raised from death, how can some of you say that the dead will not be raised to life? If that is true, it means that Christ was not raised; and if Christ has not been raised from death, then we have nothing to preach, and you have nothing to believe . . . for if the dead are not raised, neither has Christ been raised. And if Christ has not been raised, then your faith is a delusion and you are still lost in your sins' (1 Corinthians 15:12-14; 16, 17). He could hardly put it more strongly than that. He was not interested in any other theories about immortality, and we do not know what he would have said about them. It was the Christian belief he lived by and proclaimed. And that belief interpreted eternal life without any question in terms of the Resurrection of Jesus Christ.

A careful reading of the letters, however, will show that Paul did not think of the Easter event as an isolated miracle. He is not saying that because this particular man was seen alive again after his execution – glimpsed, as it were, on his way to the heavenly places – that therefore it can be assumed that this is the way ahead for each of us. His emphasis is always on the unique nature of Jesus who 'was shown with great power to be the Son of God by being raised from death' (Romans 1:4). In particular, he dwells constantly on the meaning of the crucifixion that preceded this supreme miracle. In Paul's thoughts this was not what we call a martyrdom: it was part of the story of redemption whereby the Son of God became a servant, a slave, in order to draw upon himself the entire weight of the sin and death that held the world in bondage. Paul uses many metaphors to describe what happened when Jesus went to his death, drawn from the language of Old Testament sacrifice, from courts of law, from human relations, possibly from mystery religions, and unfortunately some of these have been erected into dogmas which every Christian is required to accept. The essence of Paul's beliefs is contained in the little words 'for us'. He died 'for us' and he rose 'for us'. His death was a real death. As Günther Bornkamm says (*Paul*, Hodder & Stoughton,

1971, p. 158), 'One thing is certain: Paul means Christ's death on earth, the death he died in deepest humiliation and shame as a criminal, and not any paradoxical symbol above time.' But in that very human death Paul saw Christ drawing upon himself the sins of the whole world, accepting the last agony of the isolation and abandonment of death, going through hell for us. He even says 'God made him share our sin in order that we, in union with him, might share the righteousness of God' (2 Corinthians 5:21). It is the one of whom he could write this who had been raised from the dead. He was not speaking about a heroic figure who had been falsely condemned and surprisingly vindicated, but of one who deliberately went to the grave with the human race and was rescued with us all by the power of God. Paul knew that this was not easily grasped by the religious intellect. 'Jews want miracles for proof, and Greeks look for wisdom,' he writes (1 Corinthians 1:22-4). 'As for us, we proclaim Christ on the cross, a message that is offensive to the Jews and nonsense to the Gentiles; but for those whom God has called, both Jews and Gentiles, this message is Christ, who is the power of God and the wisdom of God.'

The Resurrection, therefore, became for Paul the pivot of his belief that the powers of death, and all that they implied, had been conquered. So we find in his letters no attempt to soften the fact of the death that awaits us all, to pretend that it is a mere incident, a happy release for the soul that has been too long confined in its bodily prison. Nothing that he writes is based on any doctrine of the immortality of the soul: for him eternal life is a matter of being raised from the dead by the same power that raised up Jesus. This is perhaps the most difficult point for us to grasp since both Christian theology and popular belief have often inculcated the idea that eternal life is indeed 'planted in the soul' and death is its liberation.

This consideration leads us right into one of the thorniest areas of Paul's thinking where the question is not only: How can I discover what he is saying about the nature of the resurrection life? But, having done so, can I accept it? The trouble is that many have tended to hear something that Paul is *not* saying and are quite vociferous in rejecting it.

There is no one statement in the Apostles' Creed that causes more offence, not only to sceptics but to ordinary Church members, than that which says: 'I believe . . . in the resurrection of the body.' It is one of these topics which a preacher can enlarge on year after year without making a dent on the views of those who think they know what it means and reject it. The words 'resurrection of the body' inevitably suggest the idea that at some time and place the component parts of our present physical bodies will be put together again, and a belief of this kind can lead to all kinds of practices and prejudices ranging from competition to have a tomb on the Mount of Olives to objection to cremation. A little reflection will also produce a crop of unanswerable questions, such as: Will I be put together as the frail, feeble old person I expect to be when I die, or will there be some process of rejuvenation? Or will a reappearance of my physical body not necessitate the provision of a physical environment and does that not lead us to some very materialistic kind of heaven? It is strange that it does not often occur to those who imagine that this is what is meant by 'the resurrection of the body' that there are quite insuperable difficulties for anyone in any age, including Paul's, in believing that the physical body is meant. For one thing, even when we are alive, the total components of our bodies are changed roughly every seven years so that there is no permanent entity to be resurrected. For another, is it likely that God would favour the old person who dies peacefully in bed and is tidily placed in a coffin and in a grave over the young person who is blown to pieces on the battlefield?

The simple solution to these unthinkable thoughts is that Paul quite explicitly declares that the Good News does not include the resurrection of this physical body we now possess. He is even quite rude about the people who ask such a question. 'Someone will ask,' he writes (1 Corinthians 15:35-8), ' "How can the dead be raised to life? What kind of body will they have?" You fool! When you plant a seed in the ground it does not sprout to life unless it dies. And what you plant in the ground is a bare seed, perhaps a grain of wheat, or of some other kind, not the full-bodied plant that will grow up. God provides that seed with the body he wishes; he gives each seed its own proper body.' After pointing out the variety of bodies in the universe from the fish and the animals to the sun, moon, and stars, he goes on (v. 42): 'This is how it will be when the dead are raised to life. When the body is buried it is mortal; when raised, it will be immortal. When buried, it is ugly and weak; when raised, it will be beautiful and strong. When buried, it is a physical body; when raised, it will be a spiritual body. There is, of course, a physical body, so there has to be a spiritual body.' He then suggests that this spiritual body will be in the likeness of Christ. 'Just as we wear the likeness of the man made of earth, so we will wear the likeness of the Man from heaven.'

Such a concept, without answering the questions that no mortal can ever answer, beautifully illuminates what Paul believes about the future state of those who are 'in Christ'. His doctrine of resurrection, far from being a crude belief compared with that of the immortality of the soul, is surely much richer and more satisfying. For it emphasizes the continuation, or rather the re-creation, of the personality with all its distinction and uniqueness. If what he calls a 'spiritual body' is almost impossible for us to envisage it is surely more comprehensible than that of an amorphous agglomeration of souls. From other passages in the letters we find Paul concerned about what he calls the 'clothing of the spirit'. He sees the spiritual body as the heavenly equivalent to the fleshly clothing we now wear. 'For we know that when this tent we live in – our body here on earth – is torn down, God will have a house in heaven for us to live in, a home he himself made, which will last forever.' Paul is too much of a realist to pretend that he would like to make the exchange right now but he finds the thought of the new 'clothing' an inspiration for this present life. 'While we live in this earthly tent we groan with a feeling of oppression; it is not that we want to get rid of our earthly body, but that we want to have the heavenly put on over us, so that what is mortal will be swallowed up by life. God is the one who has prepared us for this change, and he gave us his Spirit as the guarantee of all that he has for us.'

Paul, then, is not obsessed with the idea of heaven as those appeared to be who used to sing: 'Earth is a desert drear; heaven is my home.' But he finds in the thought of the coming resurrection a light that shines on the rough road we have to travel now. If we ask the awkward question: When does he think the end will come and he will be clothed with the spiritual body? we get different answers from his letters. Sometimes he speaks as if it were going to happen within a short time at the return of the Lord. At other times he looks forward to meeting Christ at his own death. Sometimes he seems to suggest that there is a period of sleep between the moment of death and the Last Day. At other times he seems to expect to be immediately in the presence of Christ as he dies. Such questions involving our notions of time seem less and less important today, and it is strange that where Paul is so uncertain rigid dogmas have been erected. In one moving passage Paul confesses from his prison cell that he is in two minds about whether it would be better if he were indeed to be executed. After expressing his belief that by the prayers of his friends and the help of Christ's Spirit he would be liberated, he went on: 'My deep desire and hope is that I shall never fail my duty, but that at all times, and especially right now, I shall be full of courage, so that with my whole being I shall bring honour to Christ, whether I live or die. For what is life? To me, it is Christ. Death, then, will bring more. But if by living on I can do more worthwhile work, then I am not sure which I should choose. I am caught from both sides. I want very much to leave this life and be with Christ, which is a far better thing; but it is much more important, for your sake, that I remain alive' (Philippians 1:20-4).

Nothing can better express the profound faith, the blunt honesty, the passionate love both of Christ and his churches, of this dynamic character who wore himself out carrying the Good News to every corner of the empire, dropping these letters as he went so that, in the providence of God, we can benefit from his mind and heart these two thousand years later. His final word as to what matters most in this life and the next must remain his immortal hymn to Christian love, in which he sees it as the quality into which we grow and mature, and the one possession that will last forever. 'When I was a child, my speech, feelings, and thinking were all those of a child; now that I am a man, I have no more use for childish ways. What we see now is like the dim image in a mirror; then we shall see face to face. What I know now is only partial; then it will be complete, as complete as God's knowledge of me. Meanwhile these three remain: faith, hope, and love; and the greatest of these is love' (1 Corinthians 13:11-13).

PAUL'S LETTER TO THE EPHESIANS

Ephesus, the capital of the Roman province of Asia, was a flourishing city strategically placed both militarily and commercially as a gateway from Rome to the East. The temple of Artemis, one of the seven wonders of the ancient world, was the centre of worship for the oriental peoples of the area, while the Greek city grew up alongside. Thus Ephesus was a religious, cultural, and business centre for the whole province, and an obvious place for Paul to establish a vigorous mission centre.

He stayed there about three years according to the Book of Acts, and eventually aroused violent opposition when his Gospel was seen to be undermining the religious-commercial interests of the city (Acts 19).

The letter is not an intimate one and conveys no personal greetings. For this, and other reasons, it has been conjectured that it was not originally intended exclusively for Ephesus but addressed, as it were, 'to whom it may concern'. It does not deal with specific controversies but seems rather to be a Church manifesto dealing with the essentials of Christian faith and life. We find in it tremendous statements about the Church of God's design, with its variety-in-unity; about the atoning work of Christ in whom Jew and Gentile find peace; about the working of the Spirit in the life of the Church and the individual believer. The beautiful and moving passages with which 'union in Christ' is celebrated are followed by practical advice as to the life-style of the Christian. Few of the letters speak as universally as this one, and it requires little explanation about local circumstances.

Many scholars claim that it couldn't, in this form, have been written by Paul, and that it reflects a somewhat later theology. Yet, we find in it the voice and influence of the great apostle and his understanding of the Good News. It is not possible to assign even an approximate date to the letter as we have it.

1 From Paul, who by God's will is an apostle of Christ Jesus—

To God's people who live in Ephesus, those who are faithful in their life in Christ Jesus:

[2]May God our Father and the Lord Jesus Christ give you grace and peace.

Spiritual Blessings in Christ

[3]Let us give thanks to the God and Father of our Lord Jesus Christ! For he has blessed us, in our union with Christ, by giving us every spiritual gift in the heavenly world. [4]Before the world was made, God had already chosen us to be his in Christ, so that we would be holy and without fault before him. Because of his love, [5]God had already decided that through Jesus Christ he would bring us to himself as his sons—this was his pleasure and purpose. [6]Let us praise God for his glorious grace, for the free gift he gave us in his dear Son!

[7]For by the death of Christ we are set free, that is, our sins are forgiven. How great is the grace of God, [8]which he gave to us in such large measure! In all his wisdom and insight [9]God did what he had purposed, and made known to us the secret plan he had already decided to complete by means of Christ. [10]God's plan, which he will complete when the time is right, is to bring all creation together, everything in heaven and on earth, with Christ as head.

[11]All things are done according to God's plan and decision; and God chose us to be his own people in union with Christ because of his own purpose, based on what he had decided from the very beginning. [12]Let us, then, who were the first to hope in Christ, praise God's glory!

[13]And so it was with you also: when you heard the true message, the Good News that brought you salvation, you believed in Christ, and God put his stamp of ownership on you by giving you the Holy Spirit he had

Let us praise his glory!

promised. [14]The Spirit is the guarantee that we shall receive what God has promised his people, and assures us that God will give complete freedom to those who are his. Let us praise his glory!

Paul's Prayer

[15]For this reason, ever since I heard of your faith in the Lord Jesus and your love for all God's people, [16]I have not stopped giving thanks to God for you. I remember you in my prayers, [17]and ask the God of our Lord Jesus Christ, the glorious Father, to give you the Spirit, who will make you wise and reveal God to you, so that you will know him. [18]I ask that your minds may be opened to see his light, so that you will know what is the hope to which he has called you, how rich are the wonderful blessings he promises his people, [19]and how very great is his power at work in us who believe. This power in us is the same as the mighty strength [20]which he used when he raised Christ from death, and seated him at his right side in the heavenly world. [21]Christ rules there above all heavenly rulers, authorities, powers, and lords; he is above all titles of power in this world and in the next. [22]God put all things under Christ's feet, and

gave him to the church as supreme Lord over all things.
²³The church is Christ's body, the completion of him
who himself completes all things everywhere.

From Death to Life

2 In the past you were spiritually dead because of
your disobedience and sins. ²At that time you followed the world's evil way; you obeyed the ruler of the
spiritual powers in space, the spirit who now controls
the people who disobey God. ³Actually all of us were
like them, and lived according to our natural desires,
and did whatever suited the wishes of our own bodies
and minds. Like everyone else, we too were naturally
bound to suffer God's wrath.

⁴But God's mercy is so abundant, and his love for us
is so great, ⁵that while we were spiritually dead in our
disobedience he brought us to life with Christ. It is by
God's grace that you have been saved. ⁶In our union
with Christ Jesus he raised us up with him to rule with
him in the heavenly world. ⁷He did this to demonstrate
for all time to come the extraordinary greatness of his
grace in the love he showed us in Christ Jesus. ⁸For it
is by God's grace that you have been saved, through
faith. It is not your own doing, but God's gift. ⁹There is
nothing here to boast of, since it is not the result of your
own efforts. ¹⁰God is our Maker, and in our union with
Christ Jesus he has created us for a life of good works,
which he has already prepared for us to do.

One in Christ

¹¹You Gentiles by birth—who are called the uncircumcised by the Jews, who call themselves the circumcised (which refers to what men themselves do on their
bodies)—remember what you were in the past. ¹²At that
time you were apart from Christ. You were foreigners,
and did not belong to God's chosen people. You had no
part in the covenants, which were based on God's promises to his people. You lived in this world without hope
and without God. ¹³But now, in union with Christ Jesus,
you who used to be far away have been brought near by
the death of Christ. ¹⁴For Christ himself has brought us
peace, by making the Jews and Gentiles one people.

With his own body he broke down the wall that sepa-rated them and kept them enemies. [15]He abolished the Jewish Law, with its commandments and rules, in order to create out of the two races one new people in union with himself, in this way making peace. [16]By his death on the cross Christ destroyed the enmity; by means of the cross he united both races into one body and brought them back to God. [17]So Christ came and preached the Good News of peace to all—to you Gentiles, who were far away from God, and to the Jews, who were near to him. [18]It is through Christ that all of us, Jews and Gen-tiles, are able to come in the one Spirit into the presence of the Father.

[19]So then, you Gentiles are not foreigners or strangers any longer; you are now fellow-citizens with God's peo-ple, and members of the family of God. [20]You, too, are built upon the foundation laid by the apostles and prophets, the cornerstone being Christ Jesus himself. [21]He is the one who holds the whole building together and makes it grow into a sacred temple in the Lord. [22]In union with him you too are being built together with all the others into a house where God lives through his Spirit.

Paul's Work for the Gentiles

3 For this reason I, Paul, the prisoner of Christ Jesus for the sake of you Gentiles, pray to God. [2]Surely you have heard that God, in his grace, has given me this work to do for your good. [3]God revealed his secret plan and made it known to me. (I have written briefly about this, [4]and if you will read what I have written you can learn my understanding of the secret of Christ.) [5]In past times men were not told this secret, but God has re-vealed it now by the Spirit to his holy apostles and prophets. [6]The secret is this: by means of the gospel the Gentiles have a part with the Jews in God's blessings; they are members of the same body, and share in the promise that God made in Christ Jesus.

[7]I was made a servant of the gospel by God's special gift, which he gave me through the working of his power. [8]I am less than the least of all God's people; yet God gave me this privilege of taking to the Gentiles the

Good News of the infinite riches of Christ, [9] and to make all men see how God's secret plan is to be put into effect. God, who is the Creator of all things, kept his secret hidden through all the past ages, [10] in order that at the present time, by means of the church, the angelic rulers and powers in the heavenly world might know God's wisdom, in all its different forms. [11] God did this according to his eternal purpose, which he achieved through Christ Jesus our Lord. [12] In union with him, and through our faith in him, we have the freedom to enter into God's presence with all confidence. [13] I beg you, then, do not be discouraged because I am suffering for you; it is all for your benefit.

The Love of Christ

[14] For this reason, then, I fall on my knees before the Father, [15] from whom every family in heaven and on earth receives its true name. [16] I ask God, from the wealth of his glory, to give you power through his Spirit to be strong in your inner selves, [17] and that Christ will make his home in your hearts, through faith. I pray that you may have your roots and foundations in love, [18] so that you, together with all God's people, may have the power to understand how broad and long and high and deep is Christ's love. [19] Yes, may you come to know his love—although it can never be fully known—and so be completely filled with the perfect fulness of God.

[20] To him who is able to do so much more than we can ever ask for, or even think of, by means of the power working in us: [21] to God be the glory in the church and in Christ Jesus, for all time, forever and ever! Amen.

The Unity of the Body

4 I urge you, then—I who am a prisoner because I serve the Lord: live a life that measures up to the standard God set when he called you. [2] Be humble, gentle, and patient always. Show your love by being helpful to one another. [3] Do your best to preserve the unity which the Spirit gives, by the peace that binds you together. [4] There is one body and one Spirit, just as there is one hope to which God has called you. [5] There is one

Lord, one faith, one baptism; ⁶there is one God and Father of all men, who is Lord of all, works through all and is in all.

⁷Each one of us has been given a special gift, in proportion to what Christ has given. ⁸As the scripture says,

"When he went up to the very heights
he took many captives with him;
he gave gifts to men."

⁹Now, what does "he went up" mean? It means that first he came down—that is, down to the lower depths of the earth. ¹⁰So he who came down is the same one who went up, above and beyond the heavens, to fill the whole universe with his presence. ¹¹It was he who "gave gifts to men"; he appointed some to be apostles, others to be prophets, others to be evangelists, others to be pastors and teachers. ¹²He did this to prepare all God's people for the work of Christian service, to build up the body of Christ. ¹³And so we shall all come together to that oneness in our faith and in our knowledge of the Son of God; we shall become mature men, reaching to the very height of Christ's full stature. ¹⁴Then we shall no longer be children, carried by the waves and blown about by every shifting wind of the teaching of deceitful men, who lead others to error by the tricks they invent. ¹⁵Instead, by speaking the truth in a spirit of love, we must grow up in every way to Christ, who is the head. ¹⁶Under his control all the different parts of the body fit together, and the whole body is held together by every joint with which it is provided. So when each separate part works as it should, the whole body grows and builds itself up through love.

The New Life in Christ

¹⁷In the Lord's name, then, I say this and warn you: do not live any longer like the heathen, whose thoughts are worthless, ¹⁸and whose minds are in the dark. They have no part in the life that God gives, because they are completely ignorant and stubborn. ¹⁹They have lost all feeling of shame; they give themselves over to vice, and do all sorts of indecent things without restraint.

²⁰That was not what you learned about Christ! ²¹You certainly heard about him, and as his followers you were

taught the truth that is in Jesus. ²²So get rid of your old self, which made you live as you used to—the old self that was being destroyed by its deceitful desires. ²³Your hearts and minds must be made completely new. ²⁴You must put on the new self, which is created in God's likeness, and reveals itself in the true life that is upright and holy.

Do not use harmful words

²⁵No more lying, then! Everyone must tell the truth to his brother, because we are all members together in the body of Christ. ²⁶If you become angry, do not let your anger lead you into sin; and do not stay angry all day. ²⁷Don't give the Devil a chance. ²⁸The man who used to rob must stop robbing and start working, to earn an honest living for himself, and to be able to help the poor. ²⁹Do not use harmful words in talking. Use only helpful words, the kind that build up and provide what is needed, so that what you say will do good to those who hear you. ³⁰And do not make God's Holy Spirit sad; for the Spirit is God's mark of ownership on you, a guarantee that the Day will come when God will set you free. ³¹Get rid of all bitterness, passion, and anger. No more shouting or insults. No more hateful feelings of any sort. ³²Instead, be kind and tender-hearted to one another, and forgive one another, as God has forgiven you in Christ.

Get rid of all bitterness

Living in the Light

5 Since you are God's dear children, you must try to be like him. [2]Your life must be controlled by love, just as Christ loved us and gave his life for us, as a sweet-smelling offering and sacrifice that pleases God.

[3]Since you are God's people, it is not right that any questions of immorality, or indecency, or greed should even be mentioned among you. [4]Nor is it fitting for you to use obscene, foolish, or dirty words. Rather you, should give thanks to God. [5]You may be sure of this: no man who is immoral, indecent, or greedy (for greediness is a form of idol worship) will ever receive a share in the Kingdom of Christ and of God.

[6]Do not let anyone deceive you with foolish words; it is because of these very things that God's wrath will come upon those who do not obey him. [7]So have nothing at all to do with such people. [8]You yourselves used to be in the darkness, but since you have become the Lord's people you are in the light. So you must live like people who belong to the light. [9]For it is the light that brings a rich harvest of every kind of goodness, righteousness, and truth. [10]Try to learn what pleases

the Lord. [11]Have nothing to do with the worthless things that people do, that belong to the darkness. Instead, bring them out to the light. [12](It is really too shameful even to talk about the things they do in secret.) [13]And when all things are brought out to the light, then their true nature is clearly revealed; [14]for anything that is clearly revealed becomes light. That is why it is said,

"Wake up, sleeper,
and rise from the dead!
And Christ will shine on you."

[15]So pay close attention to how you live. Don't live like ignorant men, but like wise men. [16]Make good use of every opportunity you get, because these are bad days. [17]Don't be fools, then, but try to find out what the Lord wants you to do.

[18]Do not get drunk with wine, which will only ruin you; instead, be filled with the Spirit. [19]Speak to one

Always give thanks

another in the words of psalms, hymns, and sacred songs; sing hymns and psalms to the Lord, with praise in your hearts. [20]Always give thanks for everything to God the Father, in the name of our Lord Jesus Christ.

Wives and Husbands

²¹Submit yourselves to one another, because of your reverence for Christ.

²²Wives, submit yourselves to your husbands, as to the Lord. ²³For a husband has authority over his wife in the same way that Christ has authority over the church; and Christ is himself the Saviour of the church, his body. ²⁴And so wives must submit themselves completely to their husbands, in the same way that the church submits itself to Christ.

²⁵Husbands, love your wives in the same way that Christ loved the church and gave his life for it. ²⁶He did this to dedicate the church to God, by his word, after making it clean by the washing in water, ²⁷in order to present the church to himself, in all its beauty, pure and faultless, without spot or wrinkle, or any other imperfection. ²⁸Men ought to love their wives just as they love their own bodies. A man who loves his wife loves himself. ²⁹(No one ever hates his own body. Instead, he feeds it and takes care of it, just as Christ does the church; ³⁰for we are members of his body.) ³¹As the scripture says, "For this reason, a man will leave his father and mother, and unite with his wife, and the two will become one." ³²There is a great truth revealed in this scripture, and I understand it applies to Christ and the church. ³³But it also applies to you: every husband must love his wife as himself, and every wife must respect her husband.

Children and Parents

6 Children, it is your Christian duty to obey your parents, for this is the right thing to do. ²"Honour your father and mother" is the first commandment that has a promise added: ³"so that all may be well with you, and you may live a long time in the land."

⁴Parents, do not treat your children in such a way as to make them angry. Instead, raise them with Christian discipline and instruction.

Slaves and Masters

⁵Slaves, obey your human masters, with fear and trembling; and do it with a sincere heart, as though you

were serving Christ. [6]Do this not only when they are watching you, to gain their approval; but with all your heart do what God wants, as slaves of Christ. [7]Do your work as slaves cheerfully, then, as though you served the Lord, and not merely men. [8]Remember that the Lord will reward every man, whether slave or free, for the good work he does.

[9]Masters, behave in the same way towards your slaves; and stop using threats. Remember that you and your slaves belong to the same Master in heaven, who judges everyone by the same standard.

The Whole Armour of God

[10]Finally, build up your strength in union with the Lord, and by means of his mighty power. [11]Put on all the armour that God gives you, so that you will stand up against the Devil's evil tricks. [12]For we are not fighting against human beings, but against the wicked spiritual forces in the heavenly world, the rulers, authorities, and cosmic powers of this dark age. [13]So take up God's armour now! Then when the evil day comes, you will be able to resist the enemy's attacks, and after fighting to the end, you will still hold your ground.

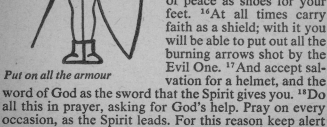

[14]So stand ready: have truth for a belt tight round your waist; put on righteousness for your breastplate, [15]and the readiness to announce the Good News of peace as shoes for your feet. [16]At all times carry faith as a shield; with it you will be able to put out all the burning arrows shot by the Evil One. [17]And accept salvation for a helmet, and the

Put on all the armour

word of God as the sword that the Spirit gives you. [18]Do all this in prayer, asking for God's help. Pray on every occasion, as the Spirit leads. For this reason keep alert and never give up; pray always for all God's people.

[19]And pray also for me, that God will give me a message, when I am ready to speak, that I may speak boldly and make known the gospel's secret. [20]For the sake of this gospel I am an ambassador, though now I am in prison. Pray that I may be bold in speaking of it, as I should.

Final Greetings

[21]Tychicus, our dear brother and faithful servant in the Lord's work, will give you all the news about me, so that you may know how I am getting along. [22]That is why I am sending him to you—to tell you how all of us are getting along, and so bring courage to your hearts.

[23]May God the Father and the Lord Jesus Christ give peace and love to all the brothers, with faith. [24]May God's grace be with all those who love our Lord Jesus Christ with undying love.

PAUL'S LETTER TO THE PHILIPPIANS

Philippi was an important city of Macedonia about ten miles from the coast. It enjoyed the prestige of a Roman colony. Readers of *Julius Caesar* will remember it as the site of the famous battle during which Mark Antony defeated the forces of Brutus and Cassius.

According to the Book of Acts (c. AD 16), Paul reached Philippi with his companions soon after he had crossed over into Europe in response to the visionary request: 'Come over to Macedonia and help us!' The church he founded there flourished and was clearly one he held in great affection. He probably came back to visit his Philippian Christians more than once and always found a joyful welcome. They do not seem to have experienced the painful divisions he found in other churches (although he does find it necessary to call two squabbling ladies to order – 4:2).

Paul is a prisoner when he writes, awaiting trial. Traditionally it has been assumed that his prison was in Rome, but arguments have been advanced in favour of Caesarea or Ephesus. The time of writing is assumed to be somewhere between AD56 and 60.

The immediate occasion of the letter seems to have been his desire to thank the Philippians for their loyalty and the gift that they had sent by the hands of Epaphroditus. The letter glows with joy in their progress in the faith and is full of personal warmth and Christian confidence. It is one of the most revealing epistles that has come down to us, and its doctrinal content springs naturally and happily from his personal testimony of what Christ has meant to him.

1 From Paul and Timothy, servants of Christ Jesus—
    To all God's people living in Philippi who are
in union with Christ Jesus, and to the church leaders
and helpers:
    ²May God our Father and the Lord Jesus Christ give
you grace and peace.

Paul's Prayer for His Readers

³I thank my God for you every time I think of you;
⁴and every time I pray for you all, I pray with joy,
⁵because of the way in which you have helped me in the
work of the gospel, from the very first day until now.
⁶And so I am sure of this: that God, who began this good
work in you, will carry it on until it is finished in the Day
of Christ Jesus. ⁷You are always in my heart! And so it
is only right for me to feel this way about you. For you
have all shared with me in this privilege that God has
given me, both now that I am in prison and also while
I was free to defend and firmly establish the gospel.
⁸God knows that I tell the truth when I say that my deep
feeling for you all comes from the heart of Christ Jesus
himself.
    ⁹This is my prayer for you: I pray that your love will
keep on growing more and more, together with true
knowledge and perfect judgment, ¹⁰so that you will be
able to choose what is best. Then you will be free from
all impurity and blame on the Day of Christ. ¹¹Your
lives will be filled with the truly good qualities which
Jesus Christ alone can produce, for the glory and praise
of God.

To Live Is Christ

¹²I want you to know, my brothers, that the things
that have happened to me have really helped the progress of the gospel. ¹³As a result, the whole palace guard
and all the others here know that I am in prison because
I am a servant of Christ. ¹⁴And my being in prison has

given most of the brothers more confidence in the Lord, so that they grow bolder all the time in preaching the message without fear.

[15]Of course some of them preach Christ because they are jealous and quarrelsome, but others preach him with all good will. [16]These do so from love, because they know that God has given me the work of defending the gospel. [17]The others do not proclaim Christ sincerely, but from a spirit of selfish ambition; they think that they will make more trouble for me while I am in prison.

[18]It does not matter! I am happy about it—just so Christ is preached in every way possible, whether from wrong or right motives. And I will continue to be happy, [19]because I know that by means of your prayers and the help which comes from the Spirit of Jesus Christ, I shall be set free. [20]My deep desire and hope is that I shall never fail my duty, but that at all times, and especially right now, I shall be full of courage, so that with my whole being I shall bring honour to Christ, whether I live or die. [21]For what is life? To me, it is Christ. Death, then, will bring more. [22]But if by living on I can do more worthwhile work, then I am not sure which I should choose. [23]I am caught from both sides. I want very much to leave this life and be with Christ, which is a far better thing; [24]but it is much more important, for your sake, that I remain alive. [25]I am sure of this, and so I know that I will stay. I will stay on with you all, to add to your progress and joy in the faith. [26]So when I am with you again you will have even more reason to be proud of me, in your life in Christ Jesus.

[27]Now, the important thing is that your manner of life be as the gospel of Christ requires, so that, whether or not I am able to go to see you, I will hear that you stand firm with one common purpose, and fight together, with only one wish, for the faith of the gospel. [28]Don't be afraid of your enemies; always be courageous, and this will prove to them that they will lose, and that you will win, because it is God who gives you the victory. [29]For you have been given the privilege of serving Christ, not only by believing in him, but also by suffering for him. [30]Now you can take

part with me in the fight. It is the same one you saw me fighting in the past and the same one I am still fighting, as you hear.

Christ's Humility and Greatness

2 Does your life in Christ make you strong? Does his love comfort you? Do you have fellowship with the Spirit? Do you feel kindness and compassion for one another? [2]I urge you, then, make me completely happy by having the same thoughts, sharing the same love, and being one in soul and mind. [3]Don't do anything from selfish ambition, or from a cheap desire to boast; but be humble towards each other, never thinking you are better than others. [4]And look out for each other's interests, not just for your own. [5]The attitude you should have is the one that Christ Jesus had:

[6] He always had the very nature of God,
   but he did not think that by force he
      should try to become equal with God.
[7] Instead, of his own free will he gave it all
   · up,
   and took the nature of a servant.
He became like man,
   and appeared in human likeness.
[8] He was humble and walked the path of
      obedience to death—
   his death on the cross.
[9] For this reason God raised him to the
      highest place above,
   and gave him the name that is greater
      than any other name.
[10] And so, in honour of the name of Jesus,
   all beings in heaven, on earth, and in the
      world below
   will fall on their knees,
[11] and all will openly proclaim that Jesus
      Christ is the Lord,
   to the glory of God the Father.

Shining as Lights in the World

[12]So then, dear friends, as you always obeyed me when I was with you, it is even more important that you

obey me now, while I am away from you. Keep on working, with fear and trembling, to complete your salvation, [13]because God is always at work in you to make you willing and able to obey his own purpose.

[14]Do everything without complaining or arguing, [15]so that you may be innocent and pure, as God's perfect children who live in a world of corrupt and sinful people. You must shine among them like stars lighting up the sky, [16]as you offer them the message of life. If you do so, I shall have reason to be proud of you on the Day of Christ, because it will show that all my effort and work have not been wasted.

[17]Perhaps my life's blood is to be poured out like an offering on the sacrifice that your faith offers to God. If that is so, I am glad, and share my joy with you all. [18]In the same way, you too must be glad and share your joy with me.

Timothy and Epaphroditus

[19]I trust in the Lord Jesus that I will be able to send Timothy to you soon, so that I may be encouraged by news of you. [20]He is the only one who shares my feelings, and who really cares about you. [21]Everyone else is concerned only about his own affairs, not about the cause of Jesus Christ. [22]And you yourselves know how he has proved his worth, how he and I, like a son and his father, have worked together for the sake of the gospel. [23]I hope to send him to you, then, as soon as I know how things are going to turn out for me. [24]And I trust in the Lord that I myself will be able to come to you soon.

[25]I have thought it necessary to send you our brother Epaphroditus, who has worked and fought by my side, and who has served as your messenger in helping me. [26]He is anxious to see you all, and is very upset because you heard that he was sick. [27]Indeed he was sick, and almost died. But God had pity on him, and not only on him but on me, too, and spared me even greater sorrow. [28]I am all the more eager, then, to send him to you, so that you will be glad again when you see him, and my own sorrow will disappear. [29]Receive him, then, with all joy, as a brother in the Lord. Show respect to all such men as he, [30]because he risked his life and nearly died,

Receive him, then, with all joy

for the sake of the work of Christ, in order to give me the help that you yourselves could not give.

The True Righteousness

3 In conclusion, my brothers, may the Lord give you much joy. It doesn't bother me to repeat what I have written before, and it will add to your safety. ²Watch out for those who do evil things, those dogs, men who insist on cutting the body. ³For we, not they, are the ones who have received the true circumcision, because we worship God by his Spirit, and rejoice in our life in Christ Jesus. We do not put any trust in external ceremonies. ⁴I could, of course, put my trust in such things. If anyone thinks he can trust in external ceremonies, I have even more reason to feel that way. ⁵I was circumcised when I was a week old. I am an Israelite by birth, of the tribe of Benjamin, a pure-blooded Hebrew. So far as keeping the Jewish Law is concerned, I was a Pharisee, ⁶and I was so zealous that I persecuted the church. So far as a man can be righteous by obeying the commands of the Law, I was without fault. ⁷But all those things that I might count as profit I now reckon as loss, for Christ's sake. ⁸Not only those things; I reckon everything as complete loss for the sake of what is so much more valuable, the knowledge of Christ Jesus my Lord.

For his sake I have thrown everything away; I consider it all as mere garbage, so that I might gain Christ, [9]and be completely united with him. No longer do I have a righteousness of my own, the kind to be gained by obeying the Law. I now have the righteousness that is given through faith in Christ, the righteousness that comes from God, and is based on faith. [10]All I want is to know Christ and to experience the power of his resurrection; to share in his sufferings and become like him in his death, [11]in the hope that I myself will be raised from death to life.

Running Towards the Goal

[12]I do not claim that I have already succeeded or have already become perfect. I keep going on to try to win the prize for which Christ Jesus has already won me to himself. [13]Of course, brothers, I really do not think that I have already won it; the one thing I do, however, is to forget what is behind me and do my best to reach what is ahead. [14]So I run straight towards the goal in order to win the prize, which is God's call through Christ Jesus to the life above.

I run straight towards the goal

[15]All of us who are spiritually mature should have this same attitude. If, however, some of you have a different attitude, God will make this clear to you. [16]However

that may be, let us go forward according to the same rules we have followed until now.

¹⁷Keep on imitating me, my brothers. We have set the right example for you, so pay attention to those who follow it. ¹⁸I have told you this many times before, and now I repeat it, with tears: there are many whose lives make them enemies of Christ's death on the cross. ¹⁹They are going to end up in hell, because their god is their bodily desires, they are proud of what they should be ashamed of, and they think only of things that belong to this world. ²⁰We, however, are citizens of heaven, and we eagerly wait for our Saviour to come from heaven, the Lord Jesus Christ. ²¹He will change our weak mortal bodies and make them like his own glorious body, using that power by which he is able to bring all things under his rule.

Instructions

4 So, then, my brothers—and how dear you are to me, and how I miss you! how happy you make me, and how proud I am of you!—this, dear brothers, is how you should stand firm in your life in the Lord.

²Euodia and Syntyche, please, I beg you, try to agree as sisters in the Lord. ³And you too, my faithful partner, I want you to help these women; for they have worked hard with me to spread the gospel, together with Clement and all my other fellow workers, whose names are in God's book of the living.

⁴May you always be joyful in your life in the Lord. I say it again: rejoice!

⁵Show a gentle attitude towards all. The Lord is coming soon. ⁶Don't worry about anything, but in all your prayers ask God for what you need, always asking him with a thankful heart. ⁷And God's peace, which is far beyond human understanding, will keep your hearts and minds safe, in union with Christ Jesus.

⁸In conclusion, my brothers, fill your minds with those things that are good and deserve praise: things that are true, noble, right, pure, lovely, and honourable. ⁹Put into practice what you learned and received from me, both from my words and from my deeds. And the God who gives us peace will be with you.

Their god is their bodily desires

Thanks for the Gift

¹⁰How great is the joy I have in my life in the Lord! After so long a time, you once more had the chance of showing that you care for me. I don't mean that you had quit caring for me—you did not have a chance to show it. ¹¹And I am not saying this because I feel neglected; for I have learned to be satisfied with what I have. ¹²I know what it is to be in need, and what it is to have more than enough. I have learned this secret, so that anywhere, at any time, I am content, whether I am full or hungry, whether I have too much or too little. ¹³I have the strength to face all conditions by the power that Christ gives me.

¹⁴But it was very good of you to help me in my troubles. ¹⁵You Philippians yourselves know very well that when I left Macedonia, in the early days of preaching the Good News, you were the only church to help me; you were the only ones who shared my profits and losses. ¹⁶More than once, when I needed help in Thessalonica, you sent it to me. ¹⁷It is not that I just want to receive gifts; rather, I want to see profit added to your account. ¹⁸Here, then, is my receipt for everything you

have given me—and it has been more than enough! I have all I need, now that Epaphroditus has brought me all your gifts. These are like a sweet-smelling offering to God, a sacrifice which is acceptable and pleasing to him. [19]And my God, with all his abundant wealth in Christ Jesus, will supply all your needs. [20]To our God and Father be the glory forever and ever. Amen.

Final Greetings

[21]Greetings to all God's people who belong to Christ Jesus. The brothers here with me send you their greetings. [22]All God's people here send greetings, especially those who belong to the Emperor's palace.

[23]May the grace of the Lord Jesus Christ be with you all.

PAUL'S LETTER TO THE COLOSSIANS

Colossae was a small market-town in Asia Minor near the cities of Hierapolis and Laodicea. Churches had been founded in the area under the leadership of Epaphras (1:7; 4:12), and Paul is this time writing to Christians he had never seen (2:1).

He writes with gratitude for all he has heard of their faith, and to assure them of his prayers. But it is obvious that he is troubled about some special dangers that threatened their Christian faith. There has been much speculation about the particular heresy that Epaphras seems to have warned Paul of when he prompted him to write this letter. We can assume that it had to do with ideas and rituals that some claimed to be all-important, thus denying the sufficiency and supremacy of Christ. For the letter rings with the affirmation of uniqueness and cosmic glory. The various kinds of Gnosticism that were current among the Colossians spoke of other authorities and other ceremonies that were necessary for salvation. Paul is concerned to proclaim the absolute authority of Christ and the liberty which he brings from all 'secret' teachings and ritual obligations.

If it is hard for us to understand the exact nature of the teachings he is attacking, we should have no difficulty in recognizing in our day of proliferating cults of all kinds the need for Christians to have these mighty reminders of the supremacy and adequacy of Christ.

This letter was probably written from the same prison as the letter to the Ephesians and around the same time (AD 56-60).

1 From Paul, who by God's will is an apostle of Christ Jesus, and from our brother Timothy—
²To God's people in Colossae, those who are our faithful brothers in Christ:
May God our Father give you grace and peace.

Prayer of Thanksgiving

³We always give thanks to God, the Father of our Lord Jesus Christ, when we pray for you. ⁴For we have heard of your faith in Christ Jesus, and of your love for all God's people. ⁵When the true message, the Good News, first came to you, you heard of the hope it offers. So your faith and love are based on what you hope for, which is kept safe for you in heaven. ⁶The gospel is bringing blessings and spreading through the whole world, just as it has among you ever since the day you first heard of the grace of God and came to know it as it really is. ⁷You learned this from Epaphras, our dear fellow servant, who is a faithful worker for Christ on our behalf. ⁸He told us of the love that the Spirit has given you.

⁹For this reason we always pray for you, ever since we heard about you. We ask God to fill you with the knowledge of his will, with all the wisdom and understanding that his Spirit gives. ¹⁰Then you will be able to live as the Lord wants, and always do what pleases him. Your lives will be fruitful in all kinds of good works, and you will grow in your knowledge of God. ¹¹May you be made strong with all the strength which comes from his glorious might, so that you may be able to endure everything with patience. ¹²And give thanks, with joy, to the Father, who has made you fit to have your share of what God has reserved for his people in the kingdom of light. ¹³He rescued us from the power of darkness and brought us safe into the kingdom of his dear Son, ¹⁴by whom we are set free, that is, our sins are forgiven.

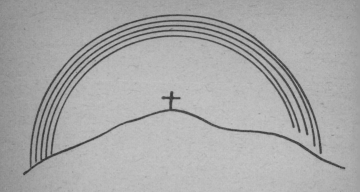

He rescued us from the power of darkness

The Person and Work of Christ

¹⁵Christ is the visible likeness of the invisible God. He is the firstborn Son, superior to all created things. ¹⁶For by him God created everything in heaven and on earth, the seen and the unseen things, including spiritual powers, lords, rulers, and authorities. God created the whole universe through him and for him. ¹⁷He existed before all things, and in union with him all things have their proper place. ¹⁸He is the head of his body, the church; he is the source of the body's life; he is the firstborn Son who was raised from death, in order that he alone might have the first place in all things. ¹⁹For it was by God's own decision that the Son has in himself the full nature of God. ²⁰Through the Son, then, God decided to bring the whole universe back to himself. God made peace through his Son's death on the cross, and so brought back to himself all things, both on earth and in heaven.

²¹At one time you were far away from God and were his enemies because of the evil things you did and thought. ²²But now, by means of the physical death of his Son, God has made you his friends, in order to bring you, holy, pure, and faultless, into his presence. ²³You must, of course, continue faithful on a firm and sure foundation, and not allow yourselves to

be shaken from the hope you gained when you heard the gospel. It is of this gospel that I, Paul, became a servant—this gospel which has been preached to everybody in the world.

Paul's Ministry to the Church

²⁴And now I am happy about my sufferings for you. For by means of my physical sufferings I help complete what still remains of Christ's sufferings on behalf of his body, which is the church. ²⁵And I have been made a servant of the church by God, who gave me this task to perform for your good. It is the task of fully proclaiming his message, ²⁶which is the secret he hid through all past ages from all mankind, but has now revealed to his people. ²⁷God's plan is this: to make known his secret to his people, this rich and glorious secret which he has for all peoples. And the secret is this: Christ is in you, which means that you will share the glory of God. ²⁸So we preach Christ to all men. We warn and teach everyone, with all possible wisdom, in order to bring each one into God's presence as a mature individual in union with Christ. ²⁹To get this done I toil and struggle, using the mighty strength that Christ supplies, which is at work in me.

2 Let me tell you how hard I have worked for you, and for the people in Laodicea, and for all those who do not know me personally. ²I do so that their hearts may be filled with courage, and that they may be drawn together in love and have the full wealth of assurance which true understanding brings. And so they will know God's secret, which is Christ himself. ³He is the key that opens all the hidden treasures of God's wisdom and knowledge.

⁴I tell you, then, do not let anyone fool you with false arguments, no matter how good they seem to be. ⁵For even though I am absent in body, yet I am with you in spirit, and I am glad as I see the resolute firmness with which you stand together in your faith in Christ.

Fulness of Life in Christ

⁶Since you have accepted Christ Jesus as Lord, live in union with him. ⁷Keep your roots deep in him, build

your lives on him, and become ever stronger in your faith, as you were taught. And be filled with thanksgiving.

⁸See to it, then, that no one makes a captive of you with the worthless deceit of human wisdom, which comes from the teachings handed down by men, and from the ruling spirits of the universe, and not from Christ. ⁹For the full content of divine nature lives in Christ, in his humanity, ¹⁰and you have been given full life in union with him. He is supreme over every spiritual ruler and authority.

He cancelled the unfavourable record

¹¹In union with him you were circumcised, not with the circumcision that is made by men, but with Christ's own circumcision, which consists of being freed from the power of this sinful body. ¹²For when you were baptized, you were buried with Christ, and in baptism you were also raised with Christ through your faith in the active power of God, who raised him from death. ¹³You were at one time spiritually dead because of your sins, and because you were Gentiles without the Law. But God has now brought you to life with Christ; God forgave us all our sins ¹⁴He cancelled the unfavourable record of our debts, with its binding rules, and did away with it completely by nailing it to the cross. ¹⁵And on that cross Christ freed himself

from the power of the spiritual rulers and authorities; he made a public spectacle of them by leading them as captives in his victory procession.

[16]So let no one make rules about what you eat or drink, or about the subject of holy days, or the new moon festival, or the Sabbath. [17]All such things are only a shadow of things in the future; the reality is Christ. [18]Do not allow yourselves to be condemned by anyone who claims to be superior because of special visions, and insists on false humility and the worship of angels. Such a person is all puffed up, for no reason at all, by his human way of thinking, [19]and has stopped holding on to Christ, who is the head. Under Christ's control the whole body is nourished and held together by its joints and ligaments, and grows as God wants it to grow.

Dying and Living with Christ

[20]You have died with Christ and are set free from the ruling spirits of the universe. Why, then, do you live as though you belonged to this world? Why do you obey such rules as [21]"Don't handle this," "Don't taste that," "Don't touch the other"? [22]All these things become useless, once they are used. They are only man-made rules and teachings. [23]Of course they appear to have wisdom in their forced worship of angels, and false humility, and severe treatment of the body; but they have no real value in controlling physical passions.

3 You have been raised to life with Christ. Set your hearts, then, on the things that are in heaven, where Christ sits on his throne at the right side of God. [2]Keep your minds fixed on things there, not on things here on earth. [3]For you have died, and your life is hidden with Christ in God. [4]Your real life is Christ, and when he appears, then you too will appear with him and share his glory!

The Old Life and the New

[5]You must put to death, then, the earthly desires at work in you, such as immorality, indecency, lust, evil passions, and greed (for greediness is a form of idol worship). [6]Because of such things God's wrath will

come upon those who do not obey him. [7]And you your-selves at one time used to live according to such desires, when your life was dominated by them.

[8]But now you must get rid of all these things: anger, passion, and hateful feelings. No insults or obscene talk must ever come from your lips. [9]Do not lie to one an-other, because you have put off the old self with its hab-its, [10]and have put on the new self. This is the new man which God, its creator, is constantly renewing in his own image, to bring you to a full knowledge of himself. [11]As a result, there are no Gentiles and Jews, circumcised and uncircumcised, barbarians, savages, slaves, or free men, but Christ is all, Christ is in all.

[12]You are the people of God; he loved you and chose you for his own. So then, you must put on compassion, kindness, humility, gentleness, and patience. [13]Be help-ful to one another, and forgive one another, whenever any of you has a complaint against someone else. You must forgive each other in the same way that the Lord has forgiven you. [14]And to all these add love, which binds all things together in perfect unity. [15]The peace that Christ gives is to be the judge in your hearts; for to this peace God has called you together in the one body. And be thankful. [16]Christ's message, in all its richness, must live in your hearts. Teach and instruct each other with all wisdom. Sing psalms, hymns, and sacred songs; sing to God, with thanksgiving in your hearts. [17]Every-thing you do or say, then, should be done in the name of the Lord Jesus, as you give thanks through him to God the Father.

Personal Relations in the New Life

[18]Wives, be obedient to your husbands, for that is what you should do as Christians.

[19]Husbands, love your wives, and do not be harsh with them.

[20]Children, it is your Christian duty to obey your parents always, for that is what pleases God.

[21]Parents, do not irritate your children, so that they will become discouraged.

[22]Slaves, obey your human masters in all things, and do it not only when they are watching you, just to gain

their approval, but do it with a sincere heart, because of your reverence for the Lord. [23]Whatever you do, work at it with all your heart, as though you were working for the Lord, and not for men. [24]Remember that the Lord will reward you; you will receive what he has kept for his people. For Christ is the real Master you serve. [25]And the wrongdoer, whoever he is, will be paid for the wrong things he does; for God judges everyone by the same standard.

4 Masters, be right and fair in the way you treat your slaves. Remember that you too have a Master in heaven.

Instructions

[2]Be persistent in prayer, and keep alert as you pray, with thanks to God. [3]At the same time pray also for us, so that God will give us a good opportunity to preach his message, to tell the secret of Christ. For that is why I am now in prison. [4]Pray, then, that I may speak in such a way as to make it clear, as I should.

[5]Be wise in the way you act towards those who are not believers, making good use of every opportunity you have. [6]Your speech should always be pleasant and interesting, and you should know how to give the right answer to everyone.

Final Greetings

[7]Our dear brother Tychicus, who is a faithful worker and fellow servant in the Lord's work, will give you all the news about me. [8]That is why I am sending him to you, to cheer you up by telling you how all of us are getting along. [9]With him goes Onesimus, the dear and faithful brother, who belongs to your group. They will tell you everything that is happening here.

[10]Aristarchus, who is in prison with me, sends you greetings, and so does Mark, the cousin of Barnabas. (You have already received instructions about him, to welcome him if he comes your way.) [11]Joshua, called Justus, also sends greetings. These three are the only Jewish converts who work with me for the Kingdom of God, and they have been a great help to me.

¹²Greetings from Epaphras, another member of your group, and a servant of Christ Jesus. He always prays fervently for you, asking God to make you stand firm, mature, and fully convinced, in complete obedience to his will. ¹³I can personally testify to his hard work for you, and for the people in Laodicea and Hierapolis. ¹⁴Luke, our dear doctor, and Demas send you their greetings.

¹⁵Give our best wishes to the brothers in Laodicea, and to Nympha and the church that meets in her house. ¹⁶After you read this letter, make sure that it is read also in the church at Laodicea. At the same time, you are to read the letter Laodicea will send you. ¹⁷And tell Archippus, "Be sure to finish the task you were given in the Lord's service."

¹⁸With my own hand I write this: *Greetings from Paul.* Do not forget my chains!

May God's grace be with you.

PAUL'S FIRST LETTER TO THE THESSALONIANS

Thessalonica was the capital of the Roman province of Macedonia. Paul came there from Philippi and soon founded a church (Acts 17). It was a 'free city' of the empire under the rule of its own magistrates. Its large and diverse population included many Jews and adherents of mystery religions.

The letters addressed to this church are the earliest documents in the New Testament and can be dated around the year AD 52. Paul was worried about the condition of the church, exposed to great pressure from rival faiths, and had sent Timothy to visit them (1 Thessalonians 3). He was relieved by his report and expresses great joy in their loyalty and love. But there were some matters on which he felt constrained to warn and advise. One of these concerned the burning question of the Lord's return – the *parousia*. The Thessalonians were clearly living in excited expectation of this event in their lifetime, and were even shocked by the fact that some of their number had died before it happened. Paul writes to reassure them that those who had died would not be excluded from the rapture of the great day. At this point he himself evidently expected the Lord's return in the immediate future. The second letter tries to damp down the excitement and restrain the wild behaviour that seems to have broken out among fanatical believers in the imminent *parousia*. Paul affirms that it cannot happen until the final act of rebellion under the 'Wicked One' (2 Thessalonians 2:3).

The apocalyptic element in these letters is stronger than in any others and this makes for difficulties in our interpretation. But they witness to the common New Testament belief in the return of Christ and warn against fanaticism in thought or recklessness in behaviour arising from this expectation. The letters also contain strong reminders of the moral duties of the Christian and the need for watchfulness. The second is much less personal and affectionate than the first, and may reflect new concerns of the apostle after getting further reports.

1 From Paul, Silas, and Timothy—
To the people of the church in Thessalonica, who belong to God the Father and the Lord Jesus Christ:
May grace and peace be yours.

The Life and Faith of the Thessalonians

[2]We always thank God for you all, and always mention you in our prayers. [3]For we remember before our God and Father how you put your faith into practice, how your love made you work so hard, and how your hope in our Lord Jesus Christ is firm. [4]We know, brothers, that God loves you and has chosen you to be his own. [5]For we brought the Good News to you, not with words only, but also with power and the Holy Spirit, and with complete conviction of its truth. You know how we lived when we were with you; it was for your own good. [6]You imitated us and the Lord; and even though you suffered much, you received the message with the joy that comes from the Holy Spirit. [7]So you became an example to all believers in Macedonia and Greece. [8]For the message about the Lord went out from you not only to Macedonia and Greece, but the news of your faith in God has gone everywhere. There is nothing, then, that we need to say. [9]All those people speak of how you received us when we visited you, and how you turned away from idols to God, to serve the true and living God

[10]and to wait for his Son to come from heaven—his Son Jesus, whom he raised from death, and who rescues us from God's wrath that is to come.

Paul's Work in Thessalonica

2 You yourselves know, brothers, that our visit to you was not a failure. [2]You know how we had already been mistreated and insulted in Philippi before we came to you in Thessalonica. Yet our God gave us courage to tell you the Good News that comes from him, even though there was much opposition. [3]The appeal we make to you is not based on error or impure motives, nor do we try to trick anyone. [4]Instead, we always speak as God wants us to, because he approved us and entrusted the Good News to us. We do not try to please men, but to please God, who tests our motives. [5]You know very well that we did not come to you with flattering talk, nor did we use words to cover up greed—God is our witness! [6]We did not try to get praise from anyone, either from you or from others, [7]even though we could have made demands on you as apostles of Christ. But we were gentle when we were with you, as gentle as a mother taking care of her children. [8]Because of our love for you we were ready to share with you not only the Good News from God but even our own lives. You were so dear to us! [9]Surely you remember, brothers, how we worked and toiled! We worked day and night so we would not be any trouble to you as we preached to you the Good News from God.

[10]You are our witnesses, and so is God: our conduct towards you who believe was pure, right, and without fault. [11]You know that we treated each one of you just as a father treats his own children. [12]We encouraged you, we comforted you, and we kept urging you to live the kind of life that pleases God, who calls you to share his own Kingdom and glory.

[13]And for this other reason, also, we always give thanks to God. When we brought you God's message, you heard it and accepted it, not as man's message but as God's message, which indeed it is. For God is at work in you who believe. [14]You, my brothers, had the same things happen to you that happened to the

churches of God in Judea, to the people there who belong to Christ Jesus. You suffered the same persecutions from your own countrymen that they suffered from the Jews, [15]who killed the Lord Jesus and the prophets, and persecuted us. How displeasing they are to God! How hostile they are to all men! [16]They even tried to stop us from preaching to the Gentiles the message that would bring them salvation. This is the last full measure of the sins they have always committed. And now God's wrath has at last fallen upon them!

Paul's Desire to Visit Them Again

[17]As for us, brothers, when we were separated from you for a little while—not in our thoughts, of course, but only in body—how we missed you and how hard we tried to see you again! [18]We wanted to go back to you. I, Paul, tried to go back more than once, but Satan would not let us. [19]After all, it is you—you, no less than others! —who are our hope, our joy, and our reason for boasting of our victory in the presence of our Lord Jesus when he comes. [20]Indeed, you are our pride and our joy!

3 Finally, we could not bear it any longer. So we decided to stay on alone in Athens [2]while we sent Timothy, our brother who works with us for God in preaching the Good News about Christ. We sent him to strengthen you and help your faith, [3]so that none of you should turn back because of these persecutions. You yourselves know that such persecutions are part of God's will for us. [4]For while we were still with you, we told you ahead of time that we were going to be persecuted; and, as you well know, that is exactly what happened. [5]That is why I had to send Timothy. I could not bear it any longer, so I sent him to find out about your faith. Surely it could not be that the Devil had tempted you, and all our work had been for nothing!

[6]Now Timothy has come back to us from you, and he has brought the welcome news about your faith and love. He has told us that you always think well of us, and that you want to see us just as much as we want to see you. [7]So, in all our trouble and suffering we have been

encouraged about you, brothers. It was your faith that encouraged us, [8]because now we really live if you stand firm in your life in the Lord. [9]Now we can give thanks to God for you. We thank him for the joy we have before our God because of you. [10]Day and night we ask him with all our heart to let us see you personally and supply what is needed in your faith.

[11]May our God and Father himself, and our Lord Jesus, prepare the way for us to come to you! [12]May the Lord make your love for one another and for all people grow more and more and become as great as our love for you. [13]In this way he will make your hearts strong, and you will be perfect and holy in the presence of our God and Father when our Lord Jesus comes with all who belong to him.

A Life that Pleases God

4 Finally, brothers, you learned from us how you should live in order to please God. This is, of course, the way you have been living. And now we beg and urge you, in the name of the Lord Jesus, to do even more. [2]For you know the instructions we gave you, by the authority of the Lord Jesus. [3]This is God's will for you: he wants you to be holy and completely free from immorality. [4]Each of you men should know how to take a wife in a holy and honourable way, [5]not with a lustful desire, like the heathen who do not know God. [6]In this matter, then, no man should do wrong to his brother or take advantage of him. We have told you this before, we strongly warned you, that the Lord will punish those who do such wrongs. [7]God did not call us to live in immorality, but in holiness. [8]So then, whoever rejects this teaching is not rejecting man, but God, who gives you his Holy Spirit.

[9]There is no need to write you about love for your fellow believers. You yourselves have been taught by God how you should love one another. [10]And you have behaved in this way towards all the brothers in all of Macedonia. So we beg you, brothers, to do even more. [11]Make it your aim to live a quiet life, to mind your own business, and earn your own living, just as we told you before. [12]In this way you will win the respect of those

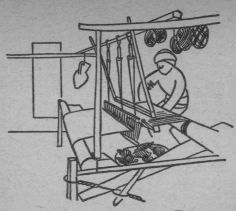

Earn your own living

who are not believers, and will not have to depend on anyone for what you need.

The Lord's Coming

¹³Brothers, we want you to know the truth about those who have died, so that you will not be sad, as are those who have no hope. ¹⁴We believe that Jesus died and rose again; so we believe that God will bring with Jesus those who have died believing in him.

¹⁵This is the Lord's teaching that we tell you: we who are alive on the day the Lord comes will not go ahead of those who have died. ¹⁶There will be the shout of command, the archangel's voice, the sound of God's trumpet, and the Lord himself will come down from heaven. Those who have died believing in Christ will rise to life first; ¹⁷then we who are living at that time will all be gathered up along with them in the clouds to meet the Lord in the air. And so we will always be with the Lord. ¹⁸So then, cheer each other up with these words.

Be Ready for the Lord's Coming

5 There is no need to write you, brothers, about the times and occasions when these things will happen. ²For you yourselves know very well that the Day of the Lord will come as a thief comes at night. ³When people say, "Everything is quiet and safe," then suddenly de-

struction will hit them! They will not escape—it will be like the pains that come upon a woman who is about to give birth. ⁴But you, brothers, are not in the darkness, and the Day should not take you by surprise like a thief. ⁵All of you are people who belong to the light, who belong to the day. We are not of the night or of the darkness. ⁶So then, we should not be sleeping, like the others; we should be awake and sober. ⁷It is at night when people sleep; it is at night when people get drunk. ⁸But we belong to the day, and we should be sober. We must wear faith and love as a breastplate, and our hope of salvation as a helmet. ⁹God did not choose us to suffer his wrath, but to possess salvation through óur Lord Jesus Christ, ¹⁰who died for us in order that we might live together with him, whether we are alive or dead when he comes. ¹¹For this reason encourage one another, and help one another, just as you are now doing.

Final Instructions and Greetings

¹²We beg you, brothers, to pay proper respect to those who work among you, those whom the Lord has chosen to guide and instruct you. ¹³Treat them with the greatest respect and love, because of the work they do. Be at peace among yourselves.

¹⁴We urge you brothers: warn the idle, encourage the timid, help the weak, be patient with all. ¹⁵See that no one pays back wrong for wrong, but at all times make it your aim to do good to one another and to all people.

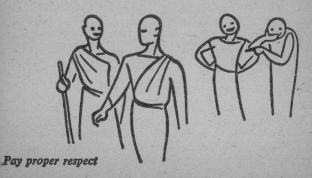

Pay proper respect

[16]Be joyful always, [17]pray at all times, [18]be thankful in all circumstances. This is what God wants of you, in your life in Christ Jesus.

[19]Do not restrain the Holy Spirit; [20]do not despise inspired messages. [21]Put all things to the test: keep what is good, [22]and avoid every kind of evil.

[23]May the God who gives us peace make you holy in every way, and keep your whole being, spirit, soul, and body, free from all fault at the coming of our Lord Jesus Christ. [24]He who calls you will do it, because he is faithful.

[25]Pray also for us, brothers.

[26]Greet all the brothers with a brotherly kiss.

[27]I urge you, by the authority of the Lord, to read this letter to all the brothers.

[28]The grace of our Lord Jesus Christ be with you.

PAUL'S SECOND LETTER TO THE THESSALONIANS

1 From Paul, Silas, and Timothy—
To the people of the church in Thessalonica, who belong to God our Father and the Lord Jesus Christ: [2]May God the Father and the Lord Jesus Christ give you grace and peace.

The Judgment at Christ's Coming

[3]We must thank God at all times for you, brothers. It is right for us to do so, because your faith is growing so much and the love each of you has for the others is becoming greater. [4]That is why we ourselves boast about you in the churches of God. We boast about the way you continue to endure and believe, through all the persecutions and sufferings you are experiencing.
[5]Here is the proof of God's righteous judgment, because as a result of all this you will become worthy of his Kingdom, for which you are suffering. [6]God will do what is right: he will bring suffering on those who make you suffer, [7]and he will give relief to you who suffer, and to us as well. He will do this when the Lord Jesus appears from heaven with his mighty angels, [8]with a flaming fire, to punish those who do not know God and those who do not obey the Good News about our Lord Jesus. [9]They will suffer the punishment of eternal destruction, separated from the presence of the Lord and from his glorious might, [10]when he comes on that Day to receive glory from all his people and honour from all who believe. You too will be among them, because you have believed the message that we told you.
[11]This is why we always pray for you. We ask our God to make you worthy of the life he called you to live. May he, by his power, fulfil all your desire for goodness and complete your work of faith. [12]In this way the name of our Lord Jesus will receive glory from you, and you from him, by the grace of our God and the Lord Jesus Christ.

The Wicked One

2 Concerning the coming of our Lord Jesus Christ and our being gathered together to be with him: I beg you, brothers, ²do not be so easily confused in your thinking or upset by the claim that the Day of the Lord has come. Perhaps this was said by someone prophesying, or by someone preaching. Or it may have been said that we wrote this in a letter. ³Do not let anyone fool you in any way. For the Day will not come until the final Rebellion takes place and the Wicked One appears, who is destined to hell. ⁴He will oppose everything which men worship and everything which men consider divine. He will put himself above them all, and even go in and sit down in God's temple and claim to be God.

⁵Don't you remember? I told you all this while I was with you. ⁶Yet there is something that keeps this from happening now, and you know what it is. At the proper time, then, the Wicked One will appear. ⁷The Mysterious Wickedness is already at work, but what is going to happen will not happen until the one who holds it back is taken out of the way. ⁸Then the Wicked One will appear, and the Lord Jesus will kill him with the breath from his mouth and destroy him with his glorious appearing, when he comes. ⁹The Wicked One will come with the power of Satan and perform all kinds of miracles and false signs and wonders, ¹⁰and use every kind of wicked deceit on those who will perish. They will perish because they did not welcome and love the truth so as to be saved. ¹¹For this reason God sends the power of error to work in them so that they believe what is false. ¹²The result is that all who have not believed the truth, but have taken pleasure in sin, will be condemned.

You Are Chosen for Salvation

¹³We must thank God at all times for you, brothers, you whom the Lord loves. For God chose you as the first to be saved, by the Spirit's power to make you God's holy people, and by your faith in the truth. ¹⁴God called you to this through the Good News we preached to you; he called you to possess your share of the glory of our

Lord Jesus Christ. ¹⁵So then, brothers, stand firm and hold on to those truths which we taught you, both in our preaching and in our letter.

¹⁶May our Lord Jesus Christ himself, and God our Father, who loved us and in his grace gave us eternal courage and a good hope, ¹⁷fill your hearts with courage and make you strong to do and say all that is good.

Pray for Us

3 Finally, brothers, pray for us, that the Lord's message may continue to spread rapidly and receive glory, just as it did among you. ²Pray also that God will rescue us from wicked and evil men. For not all people believe the message.

³But the Lord is faithful. He will make you strong and keep you safe from the Evil One. ⁴And the Lord gives us confidence in you; we are sure that you are doing and will continue to do what we tell you.

⁵May the Lord lead your hearts to the love for God and to the endurance that is given by Christ.

The Obligation to Work

⁶In the name of the Lord Jesus Christ we command you, brothers: keep away from all brothers who are living a lazy life, who do not follow the instructions that we gave them. ⁷You yourselves know very well that you should do just what we did. We were not lazy when we were with you. ⁸We did not accept anyone's support without paying for it. Instead, we worked and toiled; day and night we kept working so as not to be an expense to any of you. ⁹We did this, not because we do not have the right to demand our support; we did it to be an example for you to follow. ¹⁰While we were with you we told you, "Whoever does not want to work is not allowed to eat."

¹¹We say this because we hear that there are some people among you who live lazy lives, who do nothing except meddle in other people's business. ¹²In the name of the Lord Jesus Christ we command these people and warn them: they must lead orderly lives and work to earn their own living.

Do not treat him as an enemy

¹³But you, brothers, must not get tired of doing good. ¹⁴There may be someone there who will not obey the message we send you in this letter. If so, take note of him and have nothing to do with him, so that he will be ashamed. ¹⁵But do not treat him as an enemy; instead, warn him as a brother.

Final Words

¹⁶May the Lord himself, who is our source of peace, give you peace at all times and in every way. The Lord be with you all.

¹⁷With my own hand I write this: *Greetings from Paul.* This is the way I sign every letter; this is how I write.

¹⁸May the grace of our Lord Jesus Christ be with you all.

PAUL'S LETTER TO PHILEMON

To understand this fascinating little letter we need simply to know who Philemon and Onesimus were and why Paul was concerned about them both.

Philemon was a prosperous Christian who lived in Colossae, and Onesimus was one of his slaves who had run away, apparently after stealing some money (v. 19). Onesimus met Paul (possibly they were in the same prison) and was converted to Christ. So Paul undertakes to intercede with Philemon to forgive him and receive him back: hence this letter, which is the shortest and most intimate of the whole collection.

We find in it a glowing picture of Christianity in action and nothing reveals more clearly the warm humanity of Paul's faith. What we cannot find in it is any hint that Paul (or anyone else) was beginning to question, on Christian grounds, the institution of slavery itself. Yet, the seeds of such questioning are surely here, and the day would come when Christians revolted against the owning of one human being by another.

The letter is unquestionably by Paul himself and was written around the year AD 58. We do not know how it was received, but there is some evidence that Onesimus was later a leader in the Church and became eventually Bishop of Ephesus.

¹From Paul, a prisoner for the sake of Christ Jesus, and from our brother Timothy—

To our friend and fellow worker Philemon, ²and the church that meets in your house, and our sister Apphia, and our fellow soldier Archippus:

³May God our Father and the Lord Jesus Christ give you grace and peace.

Philemon's Love and Faith

⁴Every time I pray, brother Philemon, I mention you and give thanks to my God. ⁵For I hear of your love for all God's people and the faith you have in the Lord Jesus. ⁶My prayer is that our fellowship with you as believers will bring about a deeper understanding of every blessing which we have in our life in Christ. ⁷Your love, dear brother, has brought me great joy and much encouragement! You have cheered the hearts of all God's people.

A Request for Onesimus

⁸For this reason I could be bold enough, as your brother in Christ, to order you to do what should be done. ⁹But love compels me to make a request instead. I do this even though I am Paul, the ambassador of Christ Jesus and at present also a prisoner for his sake. ¹⁰So I make a request to you on behalf of Onesimus, who is my own son in Christ; for while in prison I have become his spiritual father. ¹¹At one time he was of no use to you, but now he is useful both to you and to me.

¹²I am sending him back to you now, and with him goes my heart. ¹³I would like to keep him here with me, while I am in prison for the gospel's sake, so that he could help me in your place. ¹⁴However, I do not want to force you to help me; rather, I would like for you to do it of your own free will. So I will not do a thing unless you agree.

¹⁵It may be that Onesimus was away from you for a short time so that you might have him back for all time.

¹⁶And now he is not just a slave, but much more than a slave: he is a dear brother in Christ. How much he means to me! And how much more he will mean to you, both as a slave and as a brother in the Lord!

Welcome him back

¹⁷So, if you think of me as your partner, welcome him back just as you would welcome me. ¹⁸If he has done you any wrong, or owes you anything, charge it to my account. ¹⁹Here, I will write this with my own hand: *I, Paul, will pay you back.* (I should not have to remind you, of course, that you owe your very life to me.) ²⁰So, my brother, please do me this favour, for the Lord's sake; cheer up my heart, as a brother in Christ!

²¹I am sure, as I write this, that you will do what I ask—in fact I know that you will do even more. ²²At the same time, get a room ready for me, because I hope that God will answer the prayers of all of you and give me back to you.

Final Greetings

²³Epaphras, who is in prison with me for the sake of Christ Jesus, sends you his greetings, ²⁴and so do my fellow workers Mark, Aristarchus, Demas, and Luke.

²⁵May the grace of the Lord Jesus Christ be with you all.

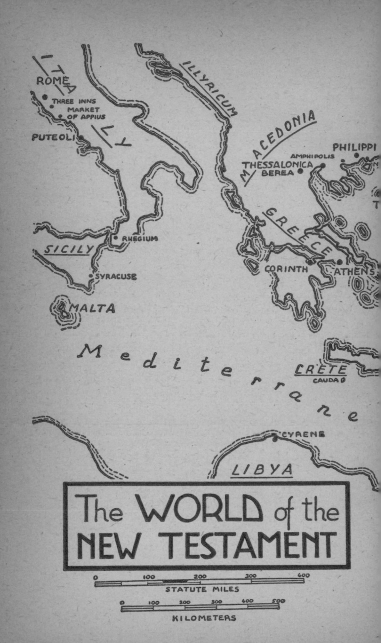

The WORLD of the
NEW TESTAMENT

Black Sea

BITHYNIA

PONTUS

GALATIA

MYSIA

CAPPADOCIA

PERGAMUM
• THYATIRA
ASIA
SMYRNA • SARDIS
PHILADELPHIA
EPHESUS
• HIERAPOLIS
• LAODICEA
• COLOSSAE
MILETUS

ANTIOCH

• ICONIUM
• LYSTRA

DERBE

TARSUS

TMOS

PAMPHYLIA

PERGA
ATTALIA
LYCIA
MYRA

CILICIA

ANTIOCH

SYRIA

CAPE SALMONE

CYPRUS

DAMASCUS

SIDON •
TYRE •

Sea

CAESAREA
JOPPA
GAZA

PALESTINE

JERUSALEM

ALEXANDRIA

EGYPT

ARABIA

THE BIBLE READING FELLOWSHIP

Readers of this commentary may wish to follow a regular pattern of Bible reading, designed to cover the Bible roughly on the basis of a book a month. Suitable Notes (send for details) with helpful exposition and prayers are provided by the Bible Reading Fellowship three times a year (January to April, May to August, September to December), and are available from:—

UK   The Bible Reading Fellowship,
St Michael's House,
2 Elizabeth Street,
London SW1.W 9RQ.

USA   The Bible Reading Fellowship,
P.O. Box 299, Winter Park,
Florida 32789,
USA.

AUSTRALIA   The Bible Reading Fellowship,
Jamieson House,
Constitution Avenue,
Reid,
Canberra, ACT 2601,
Australia.